SIPPING
Sense

Uncorking the Flavors of Wine, Entertaining and Healthy Cooking

Recipes from WINE EDUTAINMENT EXPERT
STEPHANIE BROWNE

Book design by Joana Marie Ballera

ISBN 979-8-9906009-0-4

Published by: Sipping Sense

www.sippingsense.com

Table of Contents

Foreword

Not surprisingly, my interest in wine was piqued sitting in a Boston bistro called Marché. I have always loved amazing food. Now wine was in the picture. I had obviously had wine before, but really, all I knew about it was there were two types: white and red, in that order. My mom was a scotch whiskey drinker, so I never thought about wine much before I started going to networking and work dinners. During those dinners, I got introduced to wine properly.

My love of food and entertaining started long before that evening at Marché. I did not realize that all those holiday dinners, the after-church drop-bys to my grandmother's house, and my mother's monthly bridge clubs would seal in my head vivid memories of entertaining that would mean so much later in life. Little did I know that having china plates, crystal glasses and real silver flatware were luxuries for Black families in that era. These heirlooms, passed down, are treasures. Having even one plate or bowl from your family's past can bring a smile to a table and spark a conversation.

My mother and grandmother were amazing cooks. My most vivid memories of my grandmother are in the kitchen. During my childhood, I watched her make corn pudding, rolls, coffee cake and pound cake. My grandmother was a teacher in the kitchen, always telling stories about the recipes. She would explain why she used certain ingredients or the reason why corn pudding was a staple in our family or why the pound cake was so dense. Every recipe connected to a memory. Each dish would take me on a journey through our family history.

My mother and grandmother could make anything from scratch. They rarely bought or used anything out of a can. I learned to pick out fresh vegetables and fruits in the market when I was a kid. Feeling the apples for crispness, smelling the melons for sweetness, and looking for bruises on snap peas were the norm for me. I learned early how to start with the basics: a white sauce for scalloped potatoes, herb roux for vegetables, and meringue for pies. And never use shortening in a sauce; everything tastes better with butter.

My grandmother was a master at setting a beautiful table. Every food was presented as something pretty. A china plate, a crystal bowl, or a silver tray was the norm in my home. We never ate anything out of a pan. My mom was the best at presenting yummy food and a festive environment for having fun. I knew this from the laughter and compliments I heard from the kitchen. From these two masters of food and fun, I learned that presentation matters.

Fast forward 20 years. Sitting at the table in Marché that evening, something clicked. Tasting those wines made me want to know more about why they enhanced even the most basic dish. Socializing with my friends, I realized that wine might play a part in the joyful mix of food, friends, and family.

For You!

To my friends in love with wine, food, and entertaining.

So many feel as though wine etiquette makes learning about wine and pairing it with food unapproachable. It doesn't have to be that way. It can be as easy as choosing spices for your recipe. Whether you like to cook or would rather do takeout, you can learn a few simple techniques and tricks to make appealing pairings for your palate.

Wine and food pairing should be fun. It should be all about what you like. Many people say, "I only drink white" or "I only drink red." That, to me, is limiting. With so many different grape varieties, you should never grow bored. Try as many as you can! I always say, "So many wines, so little time!"

This recipe book has been designed with a wine-pairing novice in mind. I have focused on fresh vegetables, chicken, and fish recipes to create a healthy cuisine. This conscientious approach to food pushed the boundaries of learning how to use spices, sauces, and a wine's weight, sweetness, acidity, and tannin blueprint to accomplish umami or a perfect match that delivers a sense and taste of savory yumminess. My goal is to produce umami as often as possible in my pairings.

So what does that perfect match feel like? When will you know you have achieved it? Let me describe what I believe is the feeling or sense of taste you get.

The food tastes just as you have imagined it. It's wonderful. The wine complements the food and provides balance. It doesn't overtake the food's flavors, but rather enhances them.

What is a bad pairing? I would say it's when the wine is bitter, sour, or vinegar-tasting. The food by itself may be great, but the wine throws it off. But remember, what is yummy to me may not be yummy for you. Keep exploring.

It's important to me to increase your confidence level with wine pairing after trying many of the recipes or using the wine suggestions with your own creations. Each recipe has a white and a red wine suggestion. My hope is you will try many of the pairing duos in the following pages and then expand your palate by experimenting with as many grape varieties and blends as possible. Trying different weights, levels of sweetness, acidity, and tannin in wine teaches you how different spices enhance or detract from good pairing experiences. I have also thrown in a few of the recipes passed down from my grandmother and mother to help you think about how your family's favorites deserve great wine pairings. This "ancestry alert" made selecting recipes for the book extra fun for me.

I learn every day about what makes me smile when I select wines to go with my meals. Yes, I have my favorites and my go-to grapes, but I still get excited when I stumble across a new grape on a restaurant menu or when a friend shares their favorite bottle with me. I can't help it—I'm a wine geek!

So, go on! Don't be afraid. Branch out. Try everything at least once. Share your great and not-so-great experiments with me. I, too, can be a student.

CHAPTER 1

Grape Tips for Epic Wine Experiences

Deciding how much wine to buy:

A rule of thumb is most guests will have at least two servings and one bottle will provide four 6-ounce glasses of wine. I like to have both red and white for my guests. It's a good idea to have a couple options on hand, since tastes and preferences vary from person to person.

How much wine to serve:

I would suggest doing a four-ounce pour; you can always go back for more. Although a six-ounce glass is the standard, you can start with less because you want the wine to breathe a little in the glass. Even white wines should breathe. Why?

Bottles are designed to prevent air from infiltrating the wine, so it doesn't spoil during transport and storage. Pouring a glass gives the liquid the chance to let some air in, or open up. Leaving space in your glass lets the wine open up more completely, balancing the flavors, acidity and alcohol for the best palate experience.

Choosing the right glassware:

There are many options for wine glassware. The size of the glass's bowl can enhance or detract from how your wine lands on your taste buds. A quick rule of thumb is to serve your reds and whites in an all-purpose glass. Look for one with a bowl that holds six ounces, but fill it about two-thirds to allow the wine to breathe.

Stemless Wine Glass   **Champagne Wine Glass**   **All-Purpose Wine Glass**   **Bordeaux Wine Glass**

Protocol for Serving:

My suggestion is to serve all wine between 45 and 55 degrees Fahrenheit. Remove your reds from the cooling receptacle, open, and let stand for 15–20 minutes, then serve. And remember, as soon as wine hits the air and the warmth of our hands around the glass, its temperature increases. Serving whites too cold masks the complexity the winemaker intended. It's best to serve whites right after removing them from the cooled receptacle. Reds served too warm will lose the balance of the alcohol and acidity. Have you ever had a red wine in a restaurant and the most noticeable taste was alcohol? This means the wine is being served too warm. Although it is frowned upon, I add an ice cube and cool it down.

Wine is a living organism and there are times when something goes wrong after bottling. Air can seep into the bottle and destroy the chemical balance or the wine can get too warm during transit or storage. Nothing is worse on the palate than a spoiled wine, so save your guests that experience. Always taste your wines first before serving.

How do you know it's spoiled? Here are a few tips for recognizing when wine should not be served.
- It has a strong vinegar taste and smell.
- It smells like wet cardboard and tastes bitter.
- It tastes extremely hot and like overripe raisins.

CHAPTER 2

Redefining Common Cork-y Rules

There are five taste categories called taste buds you should know and understand. Taste buds let you know what you're eating and drinking and whether it tastes "good" or "bad." This information makes eating pleasurable, which helps keep your body nourished.

The five taste senses are sweet, salty, sour, bitter, and umami. Learn your spices and flavors and experiment. The last of the five, umami, is when your taste buds experience an explosion of OMG. It's a sensation of perfection, a perfect pairing, the best combination you have ever had. Just yummy.

Wine flavors interact with your taste buds based on what they encounter first, and usually, these are the herbs, spices, or sauces used to prepare the dish.

Here are the basic tastes.

- Sweet foods mostly contain some form of sugar (sucrose, glucose, fructose, and lactose). They include foods such as honey, fruit, and ice cream.

- Salty foods contain table salt (sodium chloride) or mineral salts, such as magnesium or potassium. Think of pretzels, chips, and movie theater popcorn.

- Bitter foods may contain ingredients such as caffeine or compounds from plants, among others. Bitter is a complex taste regarding whether your taste buds recognize it as "good" or "bad." For example, some people like bitter foods, such as coffee and dark chocolate, while others don't.

- Sour foods, such as citrus fruits and vinegar, often contain some form of acid (acetic acid, citric acid, lactic acid).

- Umami is most commonly defined as "savory," but the characteristics of umami can also be described as "meaty," "complex," or even just "deliciousness." A Japanese word, umami is pronounced: "oo-ma-mee." It is found in such foods as tomatoes, asparagus, fish, mushrooms, and soy.

Taste types

Bitter

Sour

Umami

Sweet

Salty

*- Photo From
Cleveland Clinic 2023*

So what do I know about wine?

I was born in Monterey, California, which is a wine region today. How ironic! But I grew up in a middle-class Black family in Columbus, Ohio. The only wine I saw growing up was the jug bottle of Gallo Burgundy sitting in the kitchen of my Aunt Sis's home when I visited her and Uncle Gene in New York City.

As I thought about why I wanted to create this cookbook, I realized that I wished to make wine and food pairing easy! I wanted it to be less stressful than my early experiences learning to match my favorites. A few simple taste tips and a little creativity will make you a pro. I hope you find my recipes fun to make and my wine suggestions repeatable when you create your own heritage recipes inspired by family and friends.

Earlier, I talked about making yummy pairings by using a wine's weight, sweetness, acidity, and tannin levels to make wine choices that produce pleasurable palate experiences. To help you make better pairing selections, I have added my own simple pairing blueprint for you to use. This blueprint can be found in most tasting notes and the more you taste the more you will increase your confidence and ability to identify these characteristics with your own preferences and palate.

In this cookbook, I have combined my passion and experience for cooking and pairing, extending the legacy of my ancestors and my love of wine to be shared with my extended family of lovers of great food and wine.

The Pairing Blueprint

The pairing blueprint on each recipe next to my wine recommendations will give you two quick visuals to identify the weight, acidity, fruit sweetness, and tannin balance that will work with each dish. The icons below will guide your choices as you begin to experiment with wine pairings for your favorite recipes.

WINE WEIGHTS:

Light-bodied
- Low in structure, lacks deeper flavors on the palate.

Medium-bodied
- Medium structure with deeper flavors on the palate.

Full-bodied
- High structure with strong flavors on the palate.

Wine Balance Wheel:

Winemakers describe acidity, fruit sweetness, and tannin in their tasting notes. My flavor wheel is designed for a novice to identify these traditional structures simply. It indicates what you may experience "most, medium, and least" on the palate, in generalities. not percentages. What is most prominent will be the largest section on the wheel and what is the least prominent will be the smallest section.

Example:

High Acidity (Light Gray)
Medium Fruit Sweetness (Medium Gray)
Low Tannin (Dark Gray)

CHAPTER 3:

Simple Seasonings and Sauces for Sensational Sips

Wine pairing with food is all about the toppings. After you swallow a bite of that amazing dish, the toppings and spices are what remain on your palate. That's what the wine you sip complements.

The recipes in this book are a combination of tried-and-true textbook combinations and years of dishes passed down from my ancestors and yours.

Take your food and wine journey further by experimenting with all kinds of spices from every culture. Mix and match because sometimes unique combinations from different cultural cuisines break the rules and create mouth-watering umami sensations. Next time you enjoy your favorite taste, take notice.

Here are some pairing suggestions:

Sweet	Salty	Sour	Bitter
Cabernet, Port, Ice Wine, Brachetto	Cabernet, Malbec, Nero D'Avola, Merlot, Syrah, Albarino, Chardonnay	Sauvignon Blanc, Chenin Blanc, Pinot Grigio	Pinot Noir, Mourvèdre, Grenache, Sangiovese

Basic White Sauce

Ingredients

1 heaping tbsp flour
2 tbsp butter
1 cup milk
1/8 tsp salt
Sprinkle pepper

Procedure

- In a small sauce pan, melt butter on low heat. Increase heat to medium low and gradually add flour until you have a lightly browned paste, do not burn. Gradually add milk stirring constantly until the mixture bubbles.
- Turn the heat down to low and stir until sauce thickens.
- Add your favorite cheese or flavor.

Stephanie's Fish Fry Flour

Ingredients

1 cup flour
1 tbsp ground red pepper
1 tsp pepper
1 tsp salt
1 tsp garlic powder
1 tsp Slap Your Mama white pepper

Procedure

- Mix all ingredients well.

Use as a coating for fried fish or chicken.

Veggie Greens Seasoning

Ingredients

8 cloves garlic chopped
1 onion chopped
1 shallot chopped
4 tbsp olive oil
3 pkts Goya Jamon flavor
2 heaping tbsp Bajan seasoning

Procedure

- Mix all ingredients well and saute'.

Use as a base for your cooking of collard and kale greens, soups, rice, peas and beans.

Garlic Seasoning & Marinade

Ingredients

10 garlic cloves (mashed & minced)
5 black garlic cloves (mashed)
1 cup virgin olive oil

Procedure

- Place ingredients into a pottery bowl. Mix with salt and pepper. Set aside for 5 days.

Use as a base for cooking veggies, pasta and marinades. This is a great base anytime you need a little oil for sauteing.

Parmesan (Cheesy) Crusted Topping

Ingredients

1 heaping tbsp real mayonnaise
1 tbsp pesto or chimichurri
1 heaping tbsp grated Parmesan cheese

Procedure

- Mix all ingredients well.

To use as topping: spread on top of uncooked fish or chicken. Bake in 400 or low broil oven until tender and browned.*

Protein Rub

Ingredients

1 tsp red pepper flakes
1 tbsp turmeric
1 tbsp Badia Complete Seasoning
1 tsp black garlic powder
1 tsp black pepper
1 tbsp ground ginger

Procedure

- Mix all together, store in a covered container in your spice cabinet.

Rub on marinated protein, let sit for 10 minutes, grill or pan fry.

Have this rub on hand for quick and flavorful fish, poultry or meat. Great for grilling, it doesn't easily burn.

Caesar Salad Dressing

Ingredients

3-4 large garlic cloves
1/2 cup olive oil
2 rolled anchovies
1 tbsp anchovy oil
1 egg (2 for a creamier version)
Juice from 3/4 of fresh lemon
3/4 cup Parmesan cheese
Salt and pepper to taste

Procedure

- Blend garlic and oil in a blender. Add egg. Blend again. Fold in anchovies and anchovy oil and blend. Finish with cheese, salt, pepper and lemon juice and blend.

Makes about 2 cups. Store refrigerated for up to 3 weeks.

To make salad, combine 1 or 2 tbsp of dressing with chopped romaine lettuce for 4 people. Add croutons and top with anchovies and grated Parmesan cheese.

Pesto

Ingredients

3 cups basil, packed
1/2 cup pine nuts
3 garlic, cloves
Juice of 1/2 large lemon
1/2 cup Parmesan cheese
13/4 cup olive oil

Procedure

- Toast pine nuts at 300°F for 5 min. Let cool and set aside.
- Blend garlic and 1/2 cup of oil, slowly add basil, salt and pepper until smooth.
- Blend in cheese, pine nuts and lemon juice slowly until well-blended and smooth.
- Add the remaining oil.
- Chill for 30 minutes before using.

Quick true story. When I first met my husband, Basil, I made the mistake of assuming all men know how to handle a grill. I also did not know that he did not eat meat. I had spent a lot of time seasoning and marinating some baby back ribs for a cookout. I put them on the charcoal grill and then realized I needed to pick up dessert. I asked Basil to watch the ribs for 15 minutes. All he had to do was spray water on the fire if it flamed and turn the slabs. When I got back he was in a panic and my ribs were charred. I was very upset. But I married him anyway. Thirty-plus years later, he is still not allowed anywhere near the grill!

I love using my grill throughout the year. It saves lots of clean-up time before and after the meal. If you have a gas grill and a cast iron skillet, you can cook just about anything on the grill. We eat a lot of veggies, fish, and chicken in my house, so I have learned how to marinate and use all types of spices for grilling. Prep is a quick half hour and dinner can be on the table within an hour.

I also love to cook fried fish and chicken on the grill in my cast iron skillet. My secret is to use coconut oil for amazing flavor and it doesn't burn. The cast iron skillet keeps the oil hot and provides a nice browning. Another trick for cooking directly on the grill is to use copper grill mats. They are non-stick, washable, and provide even heat and even grill marks.

Nothing is better than grilled foods with wine. But it's all about the prep. Check out my herbs and seasonings recipes for great marinades.

My Spice and Oils List:

Here are my favorite brands:

Gourmet Garden Pastes

Sea Gold Butter and Olive Oil Butter

Slap Your Mama

Badia Complete Seasoning

Sazon Jamon'

Curry Powder

Refined and Unrefined Coconut Oil

Sazon Vegetable

Pesto in a Jar

Sasame Oil

Badia Black Garlic

Garlic Powder

Matouks Green Seasoning

Badia Chimichurri

Olive Oil

CHAPTER 4

Heirlooms and Heritage: Aged and Winefully Preserved

My journey through wine taught me many life lessons. When I think of how I live my life, the word legacy comes to mind. You cannot do anything in this life all by yourself. My grandmother, mother, and aunt encouraged me every step of their lives. They were my village. All were strong and involved women. Always helping others through social circles, Links, AKA, Tots and Teens or just opening their doors to the neighborhood children.

When I was seven years old, my mom became a single parent. She was now raising two children and holding down a full-time job to take care of us. Mom provided daily home-cooked meals that always included a main course and dessert even if it was only Jello with fruit cocktail. I am not sure how my mom did it, but I never heard her complain. Another tradition was to always sit down as a family with each meal. I think this also contributed to the blossoming of my entertaining bug.

Watching the women in my family cook made me learn to use the eyeball method. Nothing was measured. They would literally put the ingredients into the middle of their palms, look at it, nod their heads, and off into the bowl it would go. A pinch, a heaping spoonful, and a teacup were the methods of measuring.

Anna Helvey

Matriarch
Great-Grandmother

Anna and James Helvey

Great-Grandmother and
Great-Grandfather

Amanda and Rev. James Wood

Grandmother and Grandfather

Margaret and Clayton (Wood) Lotharp

Mom and Dad

My mother finally started to write things down as my grandmother aged. Handwritten onto any piece of paper she could find, my mother captured some of the most cherished family recipes. My mom had many of the same habits as my grandmother, except my mom was a messy cook. Flour, sugar, and chocolate stains on the recipe papers are clear evidence that she put love into the preparation. It always makes me smile, even today. Later, as the ink began to fade on some of the older recipes, I began to transfer them to cards.

The feeling I get when I make one of these recipes is so hard to describe. When I use some of the tricks and tips of my mother and grandmother, I feel their presence in the kitchen. We used to use a broom straw to test if the cake, cornbread, or casserole was done. If you insert it and it comes out clean, it's ready. What do you use today? I use a toothpick or a wooden skewer. When a bread recipe calls for rising the dough once, my grandmother would always saturate the dough in real butter and set it to rise again. Because of my memories, when I forget to buy an ingredient in a recipe, I don't panic – I check for substitutions. Many liquid and dry ingredients at hand will work! This is how you truly increase your confidence in the kitchen.

My grandmother and mother were adventurous in the kitchen. Nothing stumped them. They could take any recipe and make it their own. The legacy recipes or tips I have chosen to share in this cookbook are the ones I honed my skills with. The ones that my friends and family always ask me to share. Or they are my original and modified creations that work well paired with wines I love. I want to debunk the rules that only pair white wine with fish and vegetables and red wine with meats. I want you to learn to embrace many different white and red options in wine to pair with your dietary preferences and family favorites.

Family Dinner Table Setting

Grandmother's 1930 Sales Savings

Mom

Aunt, Amanda Wood Webb; Grandmother, Amanda Wood;
Mother, Margaret Wood Lotharp

Mom's girlfriend circle (Mother, first on the right)

Mom's Bridge
Club
(mom, 4th from
left in first row)

Uncle Gene (far
left, mom (far
left at table)
and Aunt Sis
(right at table)

Mom's Cheesy Macaroni and Cheese

SERVINGS: 6	PREP TIME: 25 MIN	COOK TIME: 90 MIN

WINE PAIRING:

Castellana Trebbiano

Los Vascos Cabernet Franc

ingredients

For the Cheese Blend (shredded or cubed):
8 oz sharp Cheddar (yellow)
4 oz sharp Cheddar (white)
4 oz Colby
1 egg beaten

For the Macaroni:
8 oz macaroni

For the White Sauce Recipe:
2 tbsp butter, melted
1 heaping tbsp flour
1 cup milk
Salt
Black pepper

30

directions

- Preheat oven to 350*. Lightly grease a medium-size casserole dish with PAM. Set aside.

- Cook macaroni according to package directions and set aside.

- In a small saucepan, melt butter on low heat. Increase heat to medium-low and gradually add flour until you have a lightly browned paste, do not burn. Gradually add milk stirring constantly until the mixture thickens and slightly bubbles.

- Add shredded or small cubed cheeses over low heat, and mix until melted.

- In a large bowl mix beaten egg into macaroni, pour macaroni and cheese sauce into greased casserole.

- Bake for 60 minutes or until thickened and browned on the edges. Serve as a side dish with your favorite protein.

Nutrition Facts	
Serves 6	
Amount Per Serving	
Calories	508
	% Daily Value*
Total Fat 30.1g	39%
Cholesterol 118.1mg	39%
Sodium 563.9mg	25%
Total Carbohydrate 34g	12%
Sugars 3.4g	
Protein 25.2g	50%

✦ *recipe notes* ✦

This comforting and cheesy macaroni and cheese is just like Mom used to make. Perfect with collard greens and fried fish or chicken

Ga Ga's Corn Pudding

| SERVINGS: 6 | PREP TIME: 15 MIN | COOK TIME: 90 MIN |

WINE PAIRING:

 Dr. Loosen Riesling

Whispering Angel Rose'

ingredients

4 ears shucked corn from the cob (fresh or frozen ears)
3/4 cup sugar
3 eggs

1 can evaporated milk
3 tbsp butter
1 heaping tbsp flour
Dash salt

directions

- Preheat oven to 350*F.

- Remove corn from cob and place in mixing bowl. Add eggs, sugar, salt, and flour to the corn and mix well. Fold in milk and mix,

- Pour corn mixture into a medium-size greased casserole dish. Cut butter into small pieces and place on top of the casserole so that it sinks into all parts of the pudding.

- Bake for 1 1/2 hours until bubbling and light brown on top. Use a tooth pick to make sure it is done. Just as in checking a cake, the toothpick should come out clean.

Nutrition Facts

Serves 6

Amount Per Serving

Calories	508
	% Daily Value*
Total Fat 30.1g	39%
Cholesterol 118.1mg	39%
Sodium 563.9mg	25%
Total Carbohydrate 34g	12%
Sugars 3.4g	
Protein 25.2g	50%

✦ *recipe notes* ✦

Indulge in Ga Ga's irresistible corn pudding, a cherished family recipe. Corn pudding is a dish that reheats quite well and can be prepared ahead of time to save time on the day you plan to serve it.

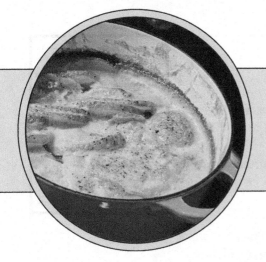

Scalloped Potatoes ala Odds & Ends

SERVINGS: 6   PREP TIME: 5 MIN   COOK TIME: 60 MIN

WINE PAIRING:

 Miner *Viognier*

 Horseshoes & Handgrenades Maison Noir *Red Blend*

ingredients

4 large Yukon Gold potatoes (sliced)
1 to 1 1/2 cups left-over cheese

For the White Sauce Recipe:
2 tbsp butter, melted
1 heaping tbsp flour
1 cup milk
Salt
Black pepper

directions

- Preheat oven to 350*F.

- Lightly spray a medium-sized baking dish with a non-stick spray and set aside.

- Clean and slice Yukon Gold potatoes and add to baking dish. You can peel the potatoes or not. I don't. It's your preference. I think the skins add flavor and they definitely add nutrients.

- Using a medium-sized saucepan, melt your butter over medium heat, add the flour, and stir until you have a slightly browned paste. Bring to a slight bubble, careful not to burn. Reduce heat to low and gradually add milk, constantly stirring to avoid lumps. Bring to a slow boil and begin adding cheeses. Keep stirring, add salt and pepper until all the cheese is melted and the sauce thickened. Remove from heat.

- Pour the cheese sauce over the potatoes and mix well. Bake for one hour or until potatoes are tender. Cheese sauce will brown around the edges and on top.

Nutrition Facts	
Serves 6	
Amount Per Serving	
Calories	298
	% Daily Value*
Total Fat 7.8g	10%
Cholesterol 20.6mg	7%
Sodium 355.5mg	15%
Total Carbohydrate 46.6g	17%
Sugars 4.2g	
Protein 11.7g	23%

✦ recipe notes ✦

Never throw away ends of great cheeses. They reappear as a wonderful surprise in scalloped potatoes. Serve with your favorite salad or as a side dish.

Mom's Broccoli Casserole

SERVINGS: 8   PREP TIME: 5 MIN   COOK TIME: 60 MIN

WINE PAIRING:

 Sun Goddess *Pinot Gris*

 Longevity *Rose'*

ingredients

2 (10oz) packages frozen chopped broccoli
2 (10oz) packages broccoli spears
2 (10oz) cans cream of chicken soup
1 cup mayonnaise

1 tsp lemon juice
1 (8oz) package grated Cheddar cheese
3/4 cup herb stuffing
1/2 cup butter

directions

- Preheat oven to 325*F.

- Cook broccoli as directed on the package and drain off all water. Cut into medium size pieces and layer in a 9x13-inch baking dish. Mix soup, mayonnaise, and lemon juice in a bowl. Spread over top of broccoli.

- In a separate bowl, mix cheese, herb stuffing, and melted butter together. Spread on top of broccoli casserole.

- Bake for 1 hour until bubbly and browned.

Nutrition Facts	
Serves 8	
Amount Per Serving	
Calories	430
	% Daily Value*
Total Fat 38.9g	50%
Cholesterol 61.3mg	20%
Sodium 592.3mg	26%
Total Carbohydrate 13.7g	5%
Sugars 2.6g	
Protein 9.3g	19%

✦*recipe notes*✦

A comforting and cheesy broccoli casserole that will remind you of home. This is nice for a buffet dinner when you are serving a big group.

Mom's Sweet Potato Casserole

SERVINGS: 6   PREP TIME: 15 MIN   COOK TIME: 90 MIN

WINE PAIRING:

 Pacific Rim Riesling

 Altaland Malbec

ingredients

For the Sweet Potato Filling:
3 large cooked sweet potatoes
3/4 stick butter
2 eggs beaten

1 1/2 cups sugar
3 tbsp cornstarch
1 cup evaporated milk
Dash cinnamon

For the Topping:
3/4 stick butter
1 cup crushed corn flakes
1/2 cup unsweetened coconut flakes
1/2 cup chopped pecans

directions

- Preheat oven to 400*F. Lightly spray a 10x15-inch baking dish with Pam and set aside.

- Boil sweet potatoes until tender. Drain, peel, mash, and place in a large mixing bowl.

- Dissolve cornstarch in mashed sweet potatoes, and add the remaining filling ingredients. Place mixture into casserole baking dish. Bake for 15 to 20 minutes until mix sets.

- In a small saucepan on low heat melt butter. Remove from heat and add remaining topping ingredients and mix well.

- Spread mixture on top of baked sweet potatoes and return to oven for another 15 minutes. The topping will become a light golden brown.

Nutrition Facts	
Serves 6	
Amount Per Serving	
Calories	625
	% Daily Value*
Total Fat 35.3g	45%
Cholesterol 122.7mg	41%
Sodium 201.5mg	9%
Total Carbohydrate 89.1g	32%
Sugars 57.6g	
Protein 8.5g	17%

✦ *recipe notes* ✦

Mom's classic sweet potato casserole is topped with a decadent pecan streusel. It's warm baked comfort on a plate. Serve as a side or dessert. Optionally, at the very end of baking, add small marshmallows on top and brown.

TEXAS CAKE

MIX IN LARGE BOWL
                               2 cups flour
                               2 cups sugar
                               1/2 teaspoon salt
                               1 teaspoon baking soda

BRING TO BOIL
                               2 sticks oleo
                               1 cup water
                               2 tablespoons cocoa

Add boiled mixture to dry ingredients all at once while hot.
Cream well, and add 2 eggs and 1/2 cup sour cream. Mix well
and pour in greased 11 x 17 x 1inch cookie sheet. Bake
20 minutes at 350 degrees. Make icing while cake is baking.
Frost while warm.

ICING

1 box powdered sugar in bowl.

BRING TO BOIL:
                               1 stick oleo
                               6 tablespoons milk
                               2 tablespoons cocoa

Add all at once to powdered sugar. Mix well
and add 1 teaspoon vanilla and 1 cup chopped
nuts (I use english walnuts).

Here's what's cookin Gr-Gr's
Coffee Cake

Recipe from: Mom   Serves: 12

2 sticks of Butter cream
1 1/4 cup sugar   well
2 eggs
Add 2 cups flour, 1 small
container sour cream, 2 tsp baking
powder, 1/2 tsp baking soda,
2 tsp vanilla.
                              over

oven temp 350°   over

Growing up in middle America in a middle-class family in the '60s and '70s meant eating most meals at home. Every dinner was planned and always had some kind of dessert. A meal was not complete without it. My mom could make a dessert out of anything. We even considered Jello made with fruit cocktail dessert.

The desserts we had repeatedly were many variations of cream pies with meringue. We would have banana cream pie, coconut cream pie, butterscotch cream pie, and chocolate cream pie. I always wondered why these were my mom's go-to desserts. But when I figured out that the ingredients for these desserts were household staples, such as sugar (white and brown), flour, milk, eggs, butter, and shortening, it all made sense. Now don't get me wrong. I loved these cream variations. They were also very pretty!

The recipes in this chapter are some of my favorites. Mostly because they all remind me of special times. For example, the pound cake or the coffee cake made by my GaGa (my grandmother) is a favorite that we would have after church when we stopped by her house before heading home for dinner. The Texas Cake my mom made was always for a large family outing. It serves about 30 people. Then, there is the bread pudding that I would beg my mom to make when I saw our white bread about to get old or we had French bread leftovers. I am sure you have a dessert that makes you smile like these do for me.

Pairing dessert with wine can be fun. You learn to love sparklings, ice wine, ports, and even dark high-tannin red wines. Try them all and see what brings a smile to your face and taste buds.

Ga Ga Cinnamon Coffee Cake

SERVINGS: 8   PREP TIME: 15 MIN   COOK TIME: 60 MIN

WINE PAIRING:

 Fonseca 10yr Port

 La Marca Sparkling Prosecco

ingredients

2 sticks butter softened
1 1/4 cups sugar
2 eggs
2 cups flour

8 oz sour cream
2 tsp baking powder
1/2 tsp baking soda
2 tsp vanilla

For the Topping:
1/4 cup sugar
1 tsp cinnamon

directions

- Preheat oven to 350*F. Grease a 9x13-inch glass or metal baking dish or bundt pan.

- Cream butter, sugar, and eggs in a mixing bowl. Add flour gradually. Mix well. Add remaining batter ingredients and stir until creamy. Set aside.

- Create topping in a small bowl. Place half of the cake batter in your baking pan. Top with the topping mixture and then add the remaining batter.

- Bake until a toothpick comes out clean. Approximately 60 minutes.

Nutrition Facts

Serves 8

Amount Per Serving

Calories	537

% Daily Value*

Total Fat 28.4g	36%
Cholesterol 117.2mg	39%
Sodium 123.6mg	5%
Total Carbohydrate 65.2g	24%
Sugars 37.8g	
Protein 7g	14%

✦*recipe notes*✦

Grandma's delightful cinnamon coffee cake is a perfect treat for brunch, dessert, or a cozy afternoon tea.

Ga Ga's Pound Cake

SERVINGS: 20-24   PREP TIME: 5 MIN   COOK TIME: 90 MIN

WINE PAIRING:

 Neige Ice Wine

 Graham Ruby Port

ingredients

4 cups flour
3 cups sugar
1 lb butter (4 sticks softened)

3/4 cup milk
6 eggs
2 tsp vanilla

directions

- Preheat oven to 350*. Grease a bundt pan and set aside.

- Make sure all ingredients are at room temperature before mixing.

- Cream butter and sugar until fluffy using a mixer on medium speed. Add one egg at a time, mixing until fluffy. Add vanilla and continue to mix. Add flour and milk gradually. Alternating each until the batter is thick and smooth. Pour batter into the pan and bake.

- Bake for 60 -75 minutes or until the top is brown and crusty.

Nutrition Facts	
Serves 20	
Amount Per Serving	
Calories	395
	% Daily Value*
Total Fat 20.1g	26%
Cholesterol 104.7mg	35%
Sodium 28.5mg	1%
Total Carbohydrate 49.7g	18%
Sugars 30.6g	
Protein 5g	10%

✦*recipe notes*✦

Ga Ga's classic pound cake, is a timeless dessert that never fails to impress. This is a decadent cake. I get caught cutting small slivers all the time. Great with a dollop of vanilla ice cream or whipped cream on top. I serve warm.

Mom's German Apple Cake

SERVINGS: 8-10   PREP TIME: 15 MIN   COOK TIME: 60 MIN

WINE PAIRING:

 Love Cork Screw *Semi-Dry Riesling*

 Lombardi *Lambrusco*

ingredients

1 cup coconut cooking oil
3 eggs
2 cups sugar
1 tsp vanilla
2 cups flour
1 tsp baking soda

1/2 tsp salt
2 tsp cinnamon
4 cups thinly sliced baking apples
1 cup chopped nuts
(walnuts or pecans) optional

For the Glaze:
1 (3 oz) pkg Philadelphia Cream Cheese
2 tbsp butter (softened)
1 1/2 cups powdered sugar
1 tsp vanilla

directions

- Preheat oven to 350*F. Grease and lightly flour a Bundt cake pan.

- For the batter:
  - Beat coconut oil and eggs together until frothy. Add sugar and vanilla and blend. In a separate bowl sift together the flour, baking soda, salt, and cinnamon.
  - Add dry ingredients to the cake batter. Mix well. Fold in apples and nuts.
  - Pour batter into pan. Bake 40-50 minutes or until a toothpick comes out clean.

- For the Icing:
  - Blend cream cheese and butter until smooth. Add vanilla and powdered sugar until smooth. Ice cake while it is hot.
  - Let cool and serve.

Nutrition Facts	
Serves 8	
Amount Per Serving	
Calories	831
	% Daily Value*
Total Fat 46.5g	60%
Cholesterol 88.1mg	29%
Sodium 364.9mg	16%
Total Carbohydrate 101.5g	37%
Sugars 74.5g	
Protein 7.6g	15%

✦ *recipe notes* ✦

A scrumptious German apple cake that combines moist cake layers with tangy apple slices. This is a tasty treat. Great for the holidays!

47

Mom's Texas Cake

SERVINGS: 20   PREP TIME: 25 MIN   COOK TIME: 40 MIN

WINE PAIRING:

 Cupcake Muscato

 **Pine & Brown** Cabernet Sauvignon

ingredients

2 cups flour
2 cups sugar
1/2 tsp salt
1 tsp baking soda
2 sticks butter

1 cup water
2 tbsp cocoa
2 eggs
1/2 cup sour cream

For the Icing:
1 stick butter
6 tbsp milk
2 tbsp cocoa
1 box powdered sugar
1 tsp vanilla
Optional: 1 cup chopped walnuts

directions

- Preheat oven to 350*F. Grease a 10x15-inch baking sheet with PAM and set aside.

- In a mixing bowl, mix flour, sugar, salt, and baking soda. Set aside. In a medium saucepan, bring butter, water, and cocoa to a boil. Add the hot mixture to the dry ingredients, and cream well. Add eggs and sour cream to the batter. Pour into greased baking sheet.

- Bake for 15-20 minutes or until the toothpick comes out clean.

- While the cake is cooking make the icing. In a saucepan, bring butter, milk, and cocoa to a boil. In a bowl, add the hot chocolate mixture to the powdered sugar, and mix well. Add vanilla and nuts. Ice the cake while both are hot.

- Let cool and serve with your favorite wine.

Nutrition Facts	
Serves 20	
Amount Per Serving	
Calories	328
	% Daily Value*
Total Fat 19.1g	25%
Cholesterol 57.1mg	19%
Sodium 137.4mg	6%
Total Carbohydrate 37.7g	14%
Sugars 26.3g	
Protein 3.7g	7%

✦*recipe notes*✦

Rich and chocolaty Texas cake, a beloved family recipe that was a staple at every celebration. This is a crowd pleaser. Better than any brownie you have ever had. Serve with vanilla ice cream.

Mom's Bread Pudding

SERVINGS: 18-20   PREP TIME: 20 MIN   COOK TIME: 60 MIN

WINE PAIRING:

 B. Stuyvesant *Champagne*

Croft *Port*

ingredients

For the Bread Soak:
3 cups day old French bread, cubed
1 1/2 cups milk
1 (12 oz) can evaporated milk
1/2 cup egg nog

For the Egg Batter:
3 eggs
1 1/2 cups sugar
1/2 cup brown sugar
2 tsp vanilla
1/4 tsp allspice

1/4 tsp cinnamon
Caramelized pecans
3 tbsp melted butter

For the Topping:
3/4 cup caramel syrup
1/2 oz whiskey (optional)

directions

- Preheat oven to 350*F.

- Soak the bread in a large mixing bowl while you make the egg batter mixture.

- Mix egg batter mixture, except the pecans and butter, in a large bowl and then add to soaked bread.

- Heat 3 tablespoons of butter in a 9x13-inch glass or metal baking dish. Spread evenly on the bottom and sides. Add the bread batter to the baking dish. Top with caramelized pecans.

- Bake for 35 to 45 minutes until a toothpick comes out clean.

- Serve and drizzle with warm caramel and whiskey sauce while hot or cold.

Nutrition Facts

Serves 20

Amount Per Serving	
Calories	331

	% Daily Value*
Total Fat 7g	9%
Cholesterol 36.6mg	12%
Sodium 42.8mg	2%
Total Carbohydrate 66.9g	24%
Sugars 64.6g	
Protein 3.7g	7%

✦*recipe notes*✦

Warm and comforting bread pudding, just like Mom used to make. This is good hot or cold. Syrup should always be served hot.

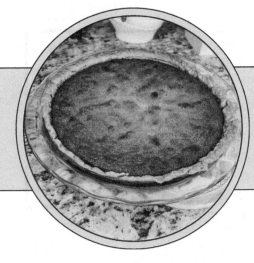

Sweet Potato Pie

SERVINGS: 8 PREP TIME: 25 MIN COOK TIME: 75 MIN

WINE PAIRING:

 Pommery *Champagne*

 Warre's Tawny *Port*

ingredients

4 large cooked yams
1 lb (4) sticks of butter
3/4 cup of granulated sugar
1 tsp vanilla
1/2 tsp of Allspice

7 eggs
2 cups whole milk
2 Pillsbury refrigerated pie crust rolled
into pie plate (not frozen)

directions

- Preheat the oven to 350*F. Recipe yields two 9-inch deep dish pies.

- Cover and boil yams until soft in the center. Cool slightly so you can handle them.

- Place butter into a mixing bowl and peel and add yams. Discard skins. Add sugar, vanilla, and Allspice. Mix well until all butter and sugar are melted.

- In a separate bowl, beat eggs and milk. Then fold into the yam mixture. Mix well and fill the pie crust with filling.

- Bake for 1 1/4 hours or until a toothpick comes out clean in middle.

✦*recipe notes*✦

A classic sweet potato pie that brings warmth and nostalgia with every bite. Serve warm with a dollop of whipped cream or a scoop of vanilla ice cream.

CHAPTER 5

Savoring the Catch, Sipping by the Shore

My family's main source of protein is fish. My husband is a pescatarian and I have learned to cook fish that tastes good, has a variety of culinary options, and can pair with wines of all weights and varietals.

This was no small feat. But I think I have mastered the art of spices, toppings, and sauces that matter when pairing wine with fish.

When the Divas traveled to South Africa to open the Nederberg Auction in 2006, I was introduced to the practice of pairing wine with the spices and sauces of a dish. And when you get this right, it creates an Umami experience.

I have spent years trying to achieve many combinations that trigger Umami on the palate. You know when you achieve this sensation. Your mouth waters and all the flavors seem to explode on your tongue. All you can say is "YUMMY!"

This chapter includes recipes that are not only healthy and taste good, but pair with all your favorite wines.

Striped Bass with Black Truffle Mushroom & Soy Sauce

SERVINGS: 4   PREP TIME: 30 MIN   COOK TIME: 30 MIN

WINE PAIRING:

 Spier Chenin Blanc

 Intruso Organic Mourvedre

ingredients

1 lb striped bass fillet (deboned and cut into 4 pieces)
10-15 shiitake mushrooms
salt
pepper
Badia Complete Seasoning

Old Bay
Juice from 1/2 fresh lime
2 tbsp butter (I use garlic butter)

For the Sauce :
1 tbsp honey
1/4 cup soy sauce
1/3 cup white wine
1 tbsp black truffle oil

directions

- Marinate cleaned fish in lime juice for 20 minutes. Remove fish and place on a plate. Season with salt, pepper, Badia Complete Seasoning, and Old Bay on both sides and set aside for 10 minutes.

- Place 1/4 cup of water and butter in a large skillet. Heat until steaming. Place fish skin side down in water, cover, and steam until tender (about 5-7 minutes). Remove fish and place on serving platter.

- Remove the remaining liquid from the skillet. Do not wash. Add sauce ingredients except for the truffle oil. Heat on high heat, constantly stirring, until blended and slightly thickened. Reduce heat, add Truffle oil, and mix. Immediately pour over the fish and serve.

Nutrition Facts	
Serves 4	
Amount Per Serving	
Calories	251
	% Daily Value*
Total Fat 12g	15%
Cholesterol 105.9mg	35%
Sodium 646.7mg	28%
Total Carbohydrate 10.7g	4%
Sugars 6.2g	
Protein 22.5g	45%

✦ *recipe notes* ✦

This satisfying and nutritious meal is quick and yummy. Serve with your favorite salad with a citrus dressing.

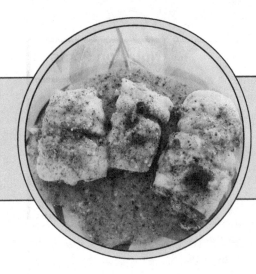

Grey Sole Stuffed with Pesto Ricotta Cheese

SERVINGS: 2   PREP TIME: 20 MIN   COOK TIME: 20 MIN

WINE PAIRING:

 Yalumba Viognier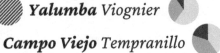

 Campo Viejo Tempranillo

ingredients

4 large sole fillets
Juice of 1/2 fresh lime
1/4 cup chives (chopped)
1 tbsp ricotta cheese

1 tbsp pesto (fresh or jar)
Old Bay
2 tbsp butter (I use garlic butter)

directions

- Preheat oven to 400*F. Prepare a baking dish with baking spray and place a piece of parchment paper on the counter.

- Wash and dry fish. Marinate in lime juice for 20 minutes.

- In a small bowl, mix cheese, pesto, and chopped chives together. Lay out the fish on the parchment paper and spread 1/2 tablespoon of cheese mixture down the middle. Roll the fish tightly and place it into the baking dish. Repeat for each piece.

- Sprinkle with Old Bay and put 1/2 tbsp of butter on top of each piece of fish.

- Bake until opaque and tender. About 10-15 minutes.

Nutrition Facts	
Serves 2	
Amount Per Serving	
Calories	232
	% Daily Value*
Total Fat 17.3g	22%
Cholesterol 75.8mg	25%
Sodium 110.8mg	5%
Total Carbohydrate 6.1g	2%
Sugars 1.3g	
Protein 14.6g	29%

✦ *recipe notes* ✦

The succulent grey sole embracing the creamy blend of pesto and ricotta cheese will leave you craving for more. You may substitute flounder, tilapia or any flat fish filets for the sole. Serve with your favorite pasta or rice.

Seafood Newburgh Casserole

SERVINGS: 6-8   PREP TIME: 20 MIN   COOK TIME: 60 MIN

WINE PAIRING:

 Love Cork Screw *Semi-Dry Riesling*

 Lombardi *Lambrusco*

ingredients

For the Newburgh Sauce:
4 heaping tbsp flour
1 stick butter
1 tsp paprika
4 cups milk
1/8 tsp salt
pepper
1/2 cup sherry
1/8 tsp red pepper flakes
(optional)

For the Seafood:
6-8 shrimp, shelled, deveined
6-8 medium scallops
1/2 lb cooked lobster meat
1/2 onion, chopped
3 garlic cloves, minced
10 shiitake mushrooms, sliced
1 tbsp butter
1/2 tbsp olive oil

For the Topping
1/2 cup seasoned bread crumbs
1/2 tsp paprika
1 tbsp butter

directions

- Preheat oven to 350*F. Grease a large casserole dish with baking spray.

- **Prepare the sauce:** In a small saucepan, melt butter on low heat. Increase heat to medium-low and gradually add flour, paprika, salt, black pepper, and red pepper flakes until you have a lightly browned paste, Do not burn! Remove from heat. In a separate saucepan, heat the milk, but do not boil. Gradually add milk to the flour mixture over low heat, stirring constantly until the mixture thickens and bubbles slightly. Remove from heat and add sherry.

- **Prepare the seafood casserole:** In a skillet, sauté olive oil, garlic, onion, and mushrooms. Drain off the liquid and set aside. In another skillet, add butter and sauté seafood until it is half done. Drain off liquid.

- **Prepare the bread crumbs:** Melt butter and add paprika and bread crumbs.

- Combine sauce and seafood in the prepared casserole dish, and top with breadcrumbs. Bake for 20-25 minutes until bubbly and browned.

Nutrition Facts	
Serves 4	
Amount Per Serving	
Calories	629
	% Daily Value*
Total Fat 33.8g	43%
Cholesterol 201.6mg	67%
Sodium 828.7mg	36%
Total Carbohydrate 40.5g	15%
Sugars 17.5g	
Protein 39.8g	80%

✦ recipe notes ✦

This comforting casserole is filled with tender seafood, velvety sauce, and a touch of flavorful magic. The cooked lobster meat may be substituted with another heavy white fish. Serve with a green vegetable or salad.

Shrimp N Grits ala Stephanie

SERVINGS: 4   PREP TIME: 25 MIN   COOK TIME: 60 MIN

WINE PAIRING:

◯ *Jermann* Pinot Grigio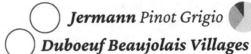

◯ **Duboeuf Beaujolais Villages**

ingredients

12-16 shrimp, shelled and deveined
Juice from 1/2 fresh lime
1/4 tsp paprika
1/4 tsp Old Bay (garlic)
1/4 tsp garlic powder
Salt and pepper to taste

1/4 tsp lemon pepper
1/4 cup white wine
1/2 cup grated Parmesan cheese
1 tbsp olive oil
Quick Grits
red pepper flakes for garnish

directions

- **For the grits:** Make Quick Grits according to package instructions for 4 servings. Add Parmesan cheese, let cheese melt, and remove from heat.

- **For the shrimp:** Season with paprika, Old Bay, and garlic powder. Marinate shrimp in lime juice for 20 minutes. In a medium skillet, add olive oil and heat on medium-high. Add shrimp, and cook until almost done. Add wine, salt, pepper and cook on medium-high until it bubbles and the shrimp are opaque.

- Divide grits among plates. Top with shrimp, gravy from the skillet, and red pepper flakes.

Nutrition Facts

Serves 4

Amount Per Serving	
Calories	207

	% Daily Value*
Total Fat 7g	9%
Cholesterol 144.9mg	48%
Sodium 504.9mg	22%
Total Carbohydrate 12.2g	4%
Sugars 0.7g	
Protein 22.3g	45%

✦ *recipe notes* ✦

Savor every spoonful of this southern comfort classic, Stephanie-Style. This dish is best with very cheesy grits. So don't be afraid to add up to a cup. I also like to use garlic olive oil butter by Sea Gold in place of regular olive oil.

Baked Cod over Whipped Sweet Potatoes

SERVINGS: 4   PREP TIME: 20 MIN   COOK TIME: 60 MIN

WINE PAIRING:

 Oyster Bay Sauvignon Blanc

 Maison Noir P-OUI (Pee Wee) Pinot Noir

ingredients

For the Cod:
4 captain cod pieces (4 oz. each)
Juice from 1/2 fresh lime
3 tbsp Sea Gold real garlic butter with olive oil
Optional: Cilantro or parsley sprigs for topping

For the Garlic Paste:
4 large garlic cloves finely chopped
1 tsp of garlic paste
1 tsp cilantro paste

For the Whipped Sweet Potatoes:
2 large sweet potatoes
1/4 cup sugar
2 tbsp Sea Gold real garlic butter with olive oil

directions

- Preheat oven to 400*F.

- Wash fish and marinate in fresh lime juice for 20 minutes. While the fish is marinating, combine garlic paste ingredients in a small bowl. Mix well.

- Place fish in a baking dish. Top each piece with garlic paste. Then top each with 1/2 tbsp of garlic butter and place the remaining garlic butter in the baking dish. Bake for 25 minutes or until the fish is flaky and the topping is browned.

- **For the whipped sweet potatoes:** Peel and cut sweet potatoes into 8 pieces. Place into a saucepan with a cup of water. Cover and steam until potatoes are soft. Drain off the remaining water. Smash potatoes with a fork, add sugar, and whip.

- Place sweet potatoes on 4 plates and top with baked cod. Top with cilantro or parsley sprigs.

Nutrition Facts	
Serves 2	
Amount Per Serving	
Calories	232
	% Daily Value*
Total Fat 17.3g	22%
Cholesterol 75.8mg	25%
Sodium 110.8mg	5%
Total Carbohydrate 6.1g	2%
Sugars 1.3g	
Protein 14.6g	29%

✦ recipe notes ✦

This is a pretty dish. The contrast of the sweet and savory from the garlic and sweet potatoes makes an Umami pairing experience. This recipe calls for garlic and cilantro paste. I use Gourmet Garden. Fresh herbs work too.

Codfish Tacos

SERVINGS: 4	PREP TIME: 15 MIN	COOK TIME: 45 MIN

WINE PAIRING:

 Martin Codax *Albarino*

Chateau Bois Redon *Bordeaux*

ingredients

1 medium avocado
1 medium tomato
8 small flour tortillas

4 medium-prepared codfish cakes

1/2 head cabbage
1/2 large onion
1/2 cup chopped sweet peppers
12 tbsp olive oil for sautéing

directions

- Dice tomato and avocado into small 1/2-inch pieces and set aside.

- Coarsely chop cabbage, pepper and onion. Sauté chopped cabbage, onion, and peppers in olive oil until tender. Set aside.

- Heat a non-stick skillet and add a tablespoon of butter or olive oil. Brown and soften the tortillas on both sides. Set them aside.

- While heating the tortillas, warm up the previously prepared codfish cakes.

- Assemble your tacos. Place crumbled pieces of half a codfish cake on each tortilla. Top with a heaping tablespoon of cabbage. Finish with your tomato and avocado relish.

Nutrition Facts	
Serves 4	
Amount Per Serving	
Calories	244
	% Daily Value*
Total Fat 13.1g	17%
Cholesterol 0mg	0%
Sodium 30.5mg	1%
Total Carbohydrate 30.6g	11%
Sugars 0.9g	
Protein 4.4g	9%

✦ *recipe notes* ✦

This recipe was created from leftovers of codfish cakes and sautéed cabbage. When I make a batch of codfish cakes there is always enough for a few days of leftovers. You can also use leftover fried or baked fish. This makes a nice filling meal.

Garlicky Cod

SERVINGS: 4   PREP TIME: 20 MIN   COOK TIME: 45 MIN

WINE PAIRING:

 Governors Bay *Sauvignon Blanc*

Casalino *Sangiovese Chianti*

ingredients

4 captain cod pieces (4 oz. each)
3 tbsp garlic butter or garlic olive
oil butter by Sea Gold
Juice of 1/2 fresh lime

For the Garlic Paste Topping:
4 large garlic cloves, finely chopped
1 tbsp pesto (fresh or prepared)
1 tsp grated Parmesan cheese
1 tbsp mayonnaise

directions

- Preheat oven to 400*F.

- Wash and marinate the fish in fresh lime juice for 20 minutes.

- While the fish is marinating, combine the garlic paste topping ingredients in a small bowl. Mix well.

- Place fish in a baking dish. Top each piece with garlic paste. Then top each with 1/2 tsp from the 3 tbsp of garlic butter or garlic olive oil butter and place the remaining butter in the baking dish.

- Bake for 25 minutes or less until the fish is flaky and the topping is browned.

Nutrition Facts	
Serves 4	
Amount Per Serving	
Calories	365
	% Daily Value*
Total Fat 8.7g	11%
Cholesterol 53.9mg	18%
Sodium 214.4mg	9%
Total Carbohydrate 47.3g	17%
Sugars 1.5g	
Protein 29.3g	59%

✦*recipe notes*✦

These tender cod fillets are infused with a burst of garlicky goodness, creating a mouthwatering dish that will make any dinner a memorable one. Serve with your favorite vegetables.

Spicy Coconut Fish & Pigeon Pea Stew

SERVINGS: 4   PREP TIME: 30 MIN   COOK TIME: 60 MIN

WINE PAIRING:

 Bogle *Petite Syrah*

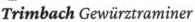 **Trimbach** *Gewürztraminer*

ingredients

1 medium leek chopped
1 medium onion chopped
3-4 garlic cloves diced
2 miniature red peppers chopped
2 miniature yellow peppers chopped

3 scallions chopped
1 tsp Slap Your Mama
1 tsp Badia Complete Seasoning
1 medium sweet potato cubed
1 packet Sazon cilantro

1 packet clam broth
4 cups vegetable stock
1 (14 oz) can diced tomatoes in juice
1 (14 oz) can pigeon peas in coconut milk
1 lb white fish (cod or halibut)
Fresh lime (for marinade)

directions

- Marinate fish in fresh lime juice while stew vegetables are cooking.

- Sauté leeks, onions, peppers, Slap Your Mama and Badia in olive oil in a large stew pot. Cook until softened. Add garlic and scallions until you smell the garlic.

- Turn off the flame and add clam broth and Sazon packet along with vegetable stock, diced tomatoes, coconut milk, and pigeon peas. Mix well, bring to a low boil on medium–high heat, reduce heat to low, and simmer for an hour.

- Cut fish into large cubes and add to hot stew mixture bring to boil until fish is tender. Turn off heat and let stand for an hour.

- Serve with hot bread.

Nutrition Facts	
Serves 4	
Amount Per Serving	
Calories	349
	% Daily Value*
Total Fat 11.2g	14%
Cholesterol 68mg	23%
Sodium 1469.5mg	64%
Total Carbohydrate 39.1g	14%
Sugars 13.5g	
Protein 25.9g	52%

✦*recipe notes*✦

Spicy stew with an explosion of flavors to pair with sweeter palate choices. Yummy. Serve with hot bread.

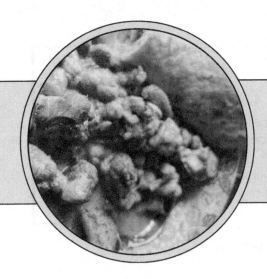

Curried Chick Pea Stew

SERVINGS: 4   PREP TIME: 30 MIN   COOK TIME: 120 MIN

WINE PAIRING:

  House of Brown *Chardonnay*

  Duckhorn *Merlot*

ingredients

1 medium onion diced
3 cloves garlic diced
2 tsp ground turmeric
1 tsp cumin
1 tsp garlic powder
2 packets Goya Jamon seasoning

1 tbsp chimichurri spice
(substitute any pepper spice of
your choosing)
3 tbsp olive oil

2 cans (15.5 oz) chickpeas, rinsed and
drained
1 can (13.5 oz) coconut milk
1 cup frozen green peas
2 cups vegetable stock
Red pepper flakes
Salt

directions

- Sauté onion, garlic, turmeric, cumin, garlic powder, Goya Jamon seasoning, chimichurri spice, and olive oil on high heat until onion is tender in a Dutch oven pot.

- Turn off the fire and add chickpeas, mix well.

- Add vegetable broth and a dash of hot red pepper flakes. Salt to taste.

- Add coconut milk and frozen peas and mix well. Cover and cook on medium–high heat for an hour, reduce heat to medium, and cook for 1 hours until chickpeas are soft. Let stand for an hour before serving.

- Serve as a vegetable entree or with your favorite fried chicken or fish.

Nutrition Facts	
Serves 4	
Amount Per Serving	
Calories	459
	% Daily Value*
Total Fat 27.4g	35%
Cholesterol 0mg	0%
Sodium 2689mg	117%
Total Carbohydrate 44.3g	16%
Sugars 4g	
Protein 15g	30%

✦ *recipe notes* ✦

This Indian influenced spiced dish complements any fried chicken or fish recipe. Use Stephanie Fish Fry Flour for a flavorful option.

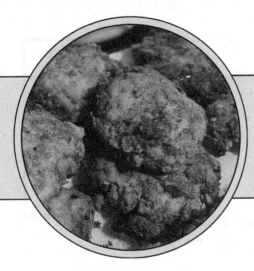

Salmon Cracker Crumb Cakes

SERVINGS: 8-10   PREP TIME: 30 MIN   COOK TIME: 45 MIN

WINE PAIRING:

  Susana Balbo *Torrontes*

  Uppercut *Cabernet Sauvignon*

ingredients

1 large (15 oz) can red salmon
2 eggs
2 large garlic cloves, minced
1/2 cup chopped yellow onions
1/4 cup chopped yellow bell peppers
1/4 cup chopped red bell peppers

10 crushed Club Crackers
Season to taste with salt, pepper, Badia
Complete, and Black garlic powder
3 tbsp flour for coating cakes
Coconut oil for frying

directions

- Place all ingredients except crackers, eggs, and salmon in a mixing bowl.

- Drain salmon and fold into veggies. Mix well.

- Beat eggs in a bowl and fold into salmon mixture.

- Fold in cracker crumbs and mix well.

- Place flour in a shallow dish.

- With your fingers grab enough mixture to form a 1 1/2 to 2-inch ball, smash/flatten into a "cake," lightly coat with flour on both sides, and place in heated coconut oil in a large, non-stick skillet. Fry until golden brown on both sides.

Nutrition Facts	
Serves 8	
Amount Per Serving	
Calories	131
	% Daily Value*
Total Fat 6.6g	8%
Cholesterol 77.8mg	26%
Sodium 336.9mg	15%
Total Carbohydrate 4.1g	1%
Sugars 1g	
Protein 12.9g	26%

✦ *recipe notes* ✦

You can use pink or red salmon in the can. Serve with your favorite green salad.

Shrimp Scampi

SERVINGS: 4   PREP TIME: 15 MIN   COOK TIME: 20 MIN

WINE PAIRING:

 Segura Vuidas *Cava Sparkling Brut*

 Longevity *Rose'*

ingredients

2 tbsp butter
2 tbsp extra-virgin olive oil
4 garlic cloves, minced
1/2 cup dry white wine

Salt, to taste
Crushed red pepper flakes, to taste
Freshly cracked black pepper, to taste
1 3/4 lbs (12-16) large shrimp, shelled &
deveined

1/3 cup chopped parsley
Freshly squeezed juice of
half a lemon

directions

- In a large skillet, heat butter with olive oil. Sauté garlic until fragrant. Add in wine, salt, pepper flakes, and cracked pepper. Let it simmer on medium-high heat until the wine is reduced to half.

- Toss in shrimp and cook on medium heat until they turn pink about 4-5 minutes per side. Take off the heat.

- Top with parsley and freshly squeezed lemon juice.

Nutrition Facts	
Serves 4	
Amount Per Serving	
Calories	314
	% Daily Value*
Total Fat 13.9g	18%
Cholesterol 334.6mg	112%
Sodium 385.7mg	17%
Total Carbohydrate 3.1g	1%
Sugars 0.5g	
Protein 40.4g	81%

✦*recipe notes*✦

Succulent shrimp takes center stage in a savory, buttery sauce, bringing together a burst of flavors that will leave you craving more. Serve with a good quality toasted crusty bread or over pasta cooked al dente.

Red Lentil Pasta with Smoked Salmon and Peas

SERVINGS: 4-6   PREP TIME: 10 MIN   COOK TIME: 30 MIN

WINE PAIRING:

 House of Brown *Rose'*

 Ceja *Medium Red Blend*

ingredients

1 pkg red lentil fusilli pasta
1 pkg smoked cooked salmon
1 cup frozen green petite peas

For the Basic White Sauce:
1 heaping tbsp flour
2 tbsp butter
1 cup milk

1/8 tsp salt
Sprinkle pepper
1/2 cup grated Parmesan cheese

directions

- Cook pasta per pkg directions. Right before the pasta is ready, drop in frozen peas and cook for 3 more minutes. Set aside 1/2 cup pasta water. Drain pasta and peas.

- Shred salmon and set aside until pasta and peas are done. Start your cheese sauce.

- **Prepare cheese sauce:** In a small saucepan, melt butter on low heat. Increase heat to medium-low and gradually add flour until you have a lightly browned paste. Do not burn. Gradually add milk stirring constantly until mixture thickens and slightly bubbles. Add Parmesan cheese and stir until melted. Turn off heat.

- Combine pasta, peas, and salmon together in your serving dish. Top with cheese sauce. If too thick, add a little of the hot pasta water. Top with grated Parmesan.

Nutrition Facts

Serves 4

Amount Per Serving	
Calories	356
	% Daily Value*
Total Fat 11.4g	15%
Cholesterol 30.2mg	10%
Sodium 876mg	38%
Total Carbohydrate 46.2g	17%
Sugars 6.3g	
Protein 20g	40%

✦ recipe notes ✦

Hearty red lentil pasta harmoniously combines with smoky salmon and vibrant peas, creating a mouthwatering and filling quick dinner. You may substitute red lentil pasta with ink, spinach or plain varieties. The red lentil is healthy and makes a pretty dish. Serve with your favorite salad.

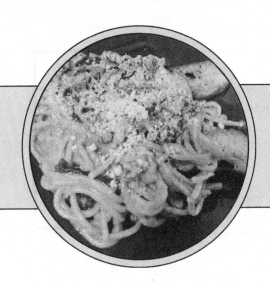

Roasted Tomato and Kale Clam Sauce with Spaghetti

SERVINGS: 4   PREP TIME: 20 MIN   COOK TIME: 20 MIN

WINE PAIRING:

 LVE *Cabernet Sauvignon*
 Chalk Hill *Chardonay*

ingredients

4 or 5 large cloves garlic minced
1 cup roasted sun-dried tomatoes, chunked
1 (10oz) package baby kale
3 tbsp olive oil

1 (15oz) can white clam sauce
1/2 (16oz) package spaghetti
1/4 cup Parmesan grated cheese
Salt and pepper to taste

directions

- Mince garlic and sauté for 2 minutes in olive oil until aromatic. Add roasted tomato pieces and kale. Cook on medium heat until soft. Add clam sauce and mix thoroughly until sauce bubbles. Turn off, and set aside.

- Cook spaghetti to your desired consistency. Drain and add to sauce. Salt and pepper to taste.

- Mix and transfer to a serving dish. Top with Parmesan cheese

Nutrition Facts	
Serves 4	
Amount Per Serving	
Calories	481
	% Daily Value*
Total Fat 35.3g	45%
Cholesterol 5.4mg	2%
Sodium 810.9mg	35%
Total Carbohydrate 32.7g	12%
Sugars 5.9g	
Protein 15.9g	32%

✦*recipe notes*✦

This Roasted Tomato and Kale Clam Sauce on a bed of spaghetti creates a comforting and healthy dish that will leave you feeling satisfied and nourished. Serve with toasted garlic bread.

Soy & Lemongrass Baked Sea Trout

SERVINGS: 4   PREP TIME: 20 MIN   COOK TIME: 30 MIN

WINE PAIRING:

 Hyland Riesling

 Radius Syrah

ingredients

1 lb fresh sea trout (arctic char or salmon can be substituted)

Juice of 1/2 fresh lime

1 tbsp lemongrass paste

1 1/2 tbsp soy sauce

1/2 tbsp grated Parmesan cheese

1 tbsp sesame seeds

2 tbsp butter

directions

- Preheat oven or grill to 375*F

- Rinse fish and place in a baking dish. Squeeze the juice of half a lime over it and add salt and pepper to taste. Let sit for 20 minutes while you make the soy paste.

- Place the soy paste ingredients (except the butter) in a small bowl. Mix. Top fish with paste and butter.

- Bake or grill for 20-25 minutes until the fish is flaky.

Nutrition Facts	
Serves 4	
Amount Per Serving	
Calories	229
	% Daily Value*
Total Fat 11g	14%
Cholesterol 82.6mg	28%
Sodium 314.9mg	14%
Total Carbohydrate 3.9g	1%
Sugars 0.8g	
Protein 24.5g	49%

✦ *recipe notes* ✦

This dish combines the Umami goodness of soy, the zesty tang of lime and lemongrass, and the tender flakiness of baked trout, creating a culinary experience that will take your taste buds on a journey. I use Gourmet Garden Lemongrass Paste. Serve with your favorite salad.

Spicy Grilled Halibut

SERVINGS: 6   PREP TIME: 40 MIN   COOK TIME: 30 MIN

WINE PAIRING:

 M. Chapoutier Grenache Blanc

Brown Estate Red Zinfandel

ingredients

2 lbs halibut
Juice of 1/2 fresh lime

For the Fish Rub:
1/2 tsp curry powder
1/2 tsp black garlic powder
1/2 tsp Badia Complete Seasoning
1/2 tsp Slap Your Mama red pepper seasoning

directions

- Preheat your outdoor grill to 400-450*F.

- Marinate fish in lime for 10 minutes.

- *For the Fish Rub:* Mix all seasonings together. Rub the mixture all over the fish after the lime marinade. Let stand for 10 minutes.

- Place fish on a non-stick grill pan or rack. Grill for 5-7 minutes on high heat on both sides until the fish is opaque and flaky. Test with your fork or skewer to see if it pierces easily. BE CAREFUL to not overcook.

- Serve immediately with a favorite vegetable.

Nutrition Facts	
Serves 6	
Amount Per Serving	
Calories	213
	% Daily Value*
Total Fat 7.6g	10%
Cholesterol 90.7mg	30%
Sodium 468.3mg	20%
Total Carbohydrate 2g	1%
Sugars 0.4g	
Protein 32.5g	65%

✦ *recipe notes* ✦

The sizzling flavors of curry powder, black garlic powder, Badia complete seasoning, and Slap your Mama red pepper seasoning create a dish that packs a punch and will leave you craving for more. This dish is best served with your favorite carb. It's nice and spicy. You can substitute "Slap Your Mama" with red pepper flakes.

Grilled Halibut with Red Chile Wine Sauce

SERVINGS: 6   PREP TIME: 40 MIN   COOK TIME: 30 MIN

WINE PAIRING:

○ **Hughes** *Picpoul de Pinet*

◍ **Brown Estate** *Primitivo*

ingredients

For the Red Chile Sauce:
1 (10oz) can diced tomatoes w/green chiles
4 tbsp butter
6 garlic cloves
1 cup fresh corn (shucked)
1/2 cup white wine
1 tsp cilantro paste or 1/2 cup fresh cilantro

For the Halibut:
1 lb halibut
Juice of 1/2 fresh lime
salt and pepper

directions

- Prepare the halibut: Marinate fish with the lime juice for about 10 minutes. Sprinkle with salt and pepper.

- Preheat grill or oven to 400*F.

- Bake or grill fish until flaky while the sauce is simmering. About 10-12 minutes.

- *Prepare the sauce:* Drain juice off tomatoes and chilies and set aside. Place butter in a medium non-stick skillet and melt on low heat. Increase heat to medium, add diced garlic, and sauté until you smell the garlic.

- Lower heat to low, add tomatoes and green chilies, and sauté until slightly bubbly. While tomatoes cook, cut corn off the cob and set aside.

- Increase heat to medium. Add white wine, salt, and pepper, and bring to a boil. Add corn and cilantro and bring to a boil again. Then reduce heat, cover, and simmer for 10 minutes. Stir occasionally. Spoon portion of sauce onto serving platter. Place cooked halibut on top of the sauce and spoon sauce on top.

✦recipe notes✦

This perfectly prepared Grilled Halibut drizzled in a tantalizing Red Chile Wine Sauce for that added kick of flavor is a perfect wine pairing dish. Serve with garlic bread for dipping in the sauce.

Nutrition Facts	
Serves 6	
Amount Per Serving	
Calories	406
	% Daily Value*
Total Fat 29g	37%
Cholesterol 89.9mg	30%
Sodium 317.3mg	14%
Total Carbohydrate 10.3g	4%
Sugars 3.4g	
Protein 23.3g	47%

CHAPTER 6:

Cluck-a-doodle-licious Winged Wine Pairings

Historically, chickens held a special importance for enslaved Black Americans, as they were the only livestock they were allowed to keep. Black domestic workers would cook fried chicken for their masters and, later, their employers. Consequently, over the years, chicken became one of the main staples for Black people, especially at Sunday dinner because it was inexpensive. Today, Blacks are still the largest consumers of chicken.

Sunday dinner has been very important as far back as slavery times because it was the only day of the week Blacks could mimic the act of being free and having the whole family come together. In addition, Saturday evening was when they received their food rations and most households did not have proper refrigeration so the food required immediate preparation.

Over the years, we have learned that fried chicken is not as healthy when prepared with many fatty oils. Therefore, chicken dishes have significantly changed to target more healthy options. If the poultry is raised properly, it is a significant source of protein for us and a wonderful part of our cultural American cuisine.

In this collection of recipes, I utilize grilling and baking with spices, rubs, and sauces from different cultures to bring out the best flavors of this American food staple and pair it with all varietals of wine.

But you don't have to give up fried chicken completely. That would be sacrilegious. Just prepare it with healthy ingredients.

Baked Chicken and Spinach Parmesan

| SERVINGS: 2 | PREP TIME: 15 MIN | COOK TIME: 45 MIN |

WINE PAIRING:

 Fetzer *Gewurztraminer*

 Vision Cellars *Pinot Noir*

ingredients

2 cups fresh spinach
2 fresh boneless chicken breasts, split
2 tbsp garlic or regular butter

Salt, black garlic, and pepper to taste
1 tbsp mayonnaise
1 tbsp grated Parmesan cheese
1/4 cup dry white wine

directions

- Preheat oven to 375*F.

- Spray a baking dish with Pam. Add garlic or regular butter in the middle of the baking dish. Spread the spinach on top. Then place the chicken on top of the spinach and cover it with spices.

- Mix mayonnaise and Parmesan cheese together in a small dish. Spread the mixture on top of the chicken.

- Bake at 375 degrees for 30-45 minutes or until chicken is tender.

- About 20 minutes in, add 1/4 cup of white wine to the dish and continue baking.

Nutrition Facts	
Serves 2	
Amount Per Serving	
Calories	250
	% Daily Value*
Total Fat 18.2g	23%
Cholesterol 55.9mg	19%
Sodium 415.2mg	18%
Total Carbohydrate 3.1g	1%
Sugars 0.2g	
Protein 8.5g	17%

✦ *recipe notes* ✦

This satisfying and nutritious meal can be prepared easily in the oven and is a complete meal in itself. A healthy one pot meal, it can be eaten alone or just add your favorite carb.

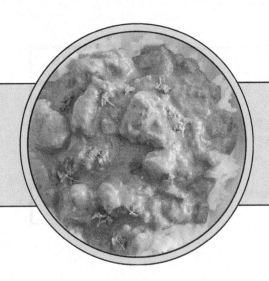

Curried Chicken with Chick & Pigeon Peas

SERVINGS: 6   PREP TIME: 60 MIN   COOK TIME: 90 MIN

WINE PAIRING:

 Chateau Ste. Michelle Riesling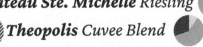
Theopolis Cuvee Blend

ingredients

For the Chicken and Marinade:
2 lbs boneless chicken breasts
1 lime for marinade
Salt
Pepper
Garlic powder
Badia Complete Seasoning

For the Frying mixture:
1 cup flour
1 tbsp ground red pepper
1 tsp black pepper
1 tsp salt
1 tsp garlic powder
Coconut oil for frying

For the Curry:
2 tbsp olive oil
1 medium onion chopped
3 to 4 garlic cloves minced
3 scallions chopped include green shoots
3 packets Goya ham seasoning
2 heaping tbsp Badia curry powder
1 (15oz) can green pigeon peas drained
1 (29oz) can chick peas drained
1 (15oz) can coconut milk

directions

Nutrition Facts		
Serves 6		
Amount Per Serving		
Calories		511
		% Daily Value*
Total Fat 21.1g		27%
Cholesterol 110.3mg		37%
Sodium 1181.4mg		51%
Total Carbohydrate 39.1g		14%
Sugars 2.9g		
Protein 42.9g		86%

- Prepare the chicken at least one hour ahead of cooking. Wash and dry boneless chicken breasts. Cut into 2-inch pieces and place in a bowl. Season with lime juice, salt, pepper, garlic powder and Badia Complete Seasoning. The lime marinade should thoroughly cover the chicken pieces.. Marinate for one hour at minimum. Overnight is OK.

- *For the curry gravy:*
   - Place onions, garlic, scallions, and seasonings into medium Dutch oven pot with olive oil and sauté until lightly browned and you can smell the garlic.
   - Add curry powder and mix. Add all the beans and coconut milk. Mix well and bring to a simmer over high heat. Reduce to low heat and cook covered for one hour. Stir occasionally to prevent sticking. The gravy is done when the beans are soft.

- While gravy is cooking, fry the chicken. Lightly dry chicken and lightly coat in flour mixture. Fry in coconut oil, browning on both sides. Cook thoroughly.

- Add chicken to curry gravy; continue cooking until tender. Let stand for 1/2 hour before serving.

✦recipe notes✦

Enjoy a flavor-packed dish of tender chicken, hearty chickpeas, and wholesome pigeon peas in a savory and spicy curry sauce. Serve with your favorite rice, naan, or roti.

Italian Spiced Grilled Boneless Chicken Thighs

SERVINGS: 4   PREP TIME: 10 MIN   COOK TIME: 25 MIN

WINE PAIRING:

 Olema *Rosé*

 1858 *Merlot*

ingredients

4 boneless chicken thighs
1/2 cup of Italian salad dressing

Black pepper
Garlic powder

directions

- Preheat the grill to medium-heat.

- Wash the chicken and dry off. Place pepper and garlic on both sides and place in a plastic storage bag. Add Italian dressing marinade to bag of chicken thighs and set aside in the refrigerator for 20 minutes before grilling.

- Grill on medium-high heat until golden and tender – approximately 20-25 minutes per side. Cook evenly on both sides.

Nutrition Facts	
Serves 4	
Amount Per Serving	
Calories	196
	% Daily Value*
Total Fat 6.4g	8%
Cholesterol 140.6mg	47%
Sodium 467.8mg	20%
Total Carbohydrate 2.9g	1%
Sugars 2.6g	
Protein 29.7g	59%

✦ *recipe notes* ✦

Fire up the grill for these chicken thighs infused with aromatic Italian flavors. Serve with your favorite green salad with a vinaigrette dressing. This is an easy summer dish.

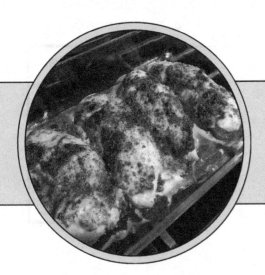

Parmesan and Chimichurri or Pesto-Crusted Chicken Breast

SERVINGS: 4   PREP TIME: 35 MIN   COOK TIME: 60 MIN

WINE PAIRING:

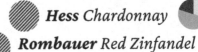

Hess *Chardonnay*

Rombauer *Red Zinfandel*

---

ingredients

For the Topping:
2 tbsp mayonnaise
1 tbsp chimichurri sauce
1 tbsp pesto
1/4 cup grated Parmesan cheese

2 tbsp garlic butter
4 chicken breast fillets
1 lime for marinade
salt
black pepper

directions

- Preheat oven to 400*F.

- Mix all topping ingredients in a small bowl. Set aside.

- Prepare chicken by marinating in fresh lime juice for 20 minutes. Season with salt, pepper, and garlic powder.

- Place in a non-stick baking dish and top with mixture. Spread paste thoroughly. Add 1/2 tbsp of butter on top of each fillet.

- Bake uncovered for 45 minutes until tender and the topping is golden brown. Increase heat for browning if needed. Don't overcook!

Nutrition Facts	
Serves 4	
Amount Per Serving	
Calories	310
	% Daily Value*
Total Fat 14.2g	18%
Cholesterol 130.6mg	44%
Sodium 281.9mg	12%
Total Carbohydrate 2.1g	1%
Sugars 0.3g	
Protein 40.9g	82%

✦ *recipe notes* ✦

Delight in crispy, flavorful goodness with this spicy protein dish. It is great with rice or potatoes. You can substitute your favorite white fish for the chicken.

Teriyaki Chicken Wings

SERVINGS: 4   PREP TIME: 10 MIN   COOK TIME: 60 MIN

WINE PAIRING:

Imagery Sauvignon Blanc

Longevity Cabernet Sauvignon

ingredients

For the Sauce:
3/4 cup soy sauce
1/4 cup honey
2 garlic cloves diced
Salt and pepper to taste

For the Chicken:
8 medium-size full chicken wings
Salt
Black pepper
Adobo poultry seasoning

directions

- Preheat oven to 375*F.

- **For the sauce:** Mix all ingredients in a bowl and set aside.

- Clean chicken wings thoroughly, place in a bowl, and season with the spices..

- Place chicken in a covered baking dish and bake for 60 minutes.

- After 40 minutes, remove the cover and coat each piece with the sauce, Return to the oven and bake uncovered for the remaining 20 mins. Chicken is done when a fork or knife pierces the meaty part of the wing easily.

Nutrition Facts

Serves 4

Amount Per Serving

Calories	517
	% Daily Value*
Total Fat 27.7g	36%
Cholesterol 237.5mg	79%
Sodium 1728.9mg	75%
Total Carbohydrate 24.8g	9%
Sugars 19.9g	
Protein 41.3g	83%

✦ *recipe notes* ✦

Finger-licking good chicken wings glazed in sweet and savory teriyaki sauce. These wings are great as an appetizer or part of a full dinner option.

CHAPTER 7

Vibrant Vegetarian Fare for All Your Vine Faves

Living with a Vegetarian/Pescatarian can be challenging when you grew up on meat and potatoes. And we boiled every vegetable until there wasn't any taste or texture left. Yes, you can. LAUGH OUT LOUD.

When I first met my husband of 30 plus years, I was surprised that this larger-than-life man only ate veggies and fish for the most part and could not cook a lick. If you want to end up with something edible, you don't want him anywhere near the kitchen!

Remember, he burned my ribs at one of the first social gatherings that we hosted together.

Over time I have learned that veggies can be very tasty, with all levels of texture and complexity. And you can add so many spices, sauces, cheeses, and non-meat proteins to dishes that you would be surprised to discover that most of my dishes don't contain any meat or poultry.

I have friends who once turned their noses up at all veggie meals but now enjoy my veggie and wine pairings.

Here are a few tips I have learned along the way with veggies:

- Don't overcook your veggies. Leave a little snap in them. They should not change color.
- Garlic, Garlic, Garlic.
- Mix sweet and savory together. They pair better with wine.
- Veggies with texture can substitute for meats.
- Try many different kinds of cheese with your veggies to help with wine pairing possibilities.

Use your veggies, herbs, and spices to excite your tastebuds or add to your favorite legumes.

There is a whole new world out there if you let veggies rule.

Linguini with Pesto & Shiitake Mushrooms

SERVINGS: 2-4   PREP TIME: 10 MIN   COOK TIME: 20 MIN

WINE PAIRING:

 Oak Grove *Viognier*

Primus *Bordeaux Blend*

ingredients

8 oz linguini pasta (1/2 box)
2 tbsp fresh or pre-made pesto
1 package fresh shiitake mushrooms sliced (8 oz)

2 garlic cloves diced
2 tbsp olive oil
1/4 cup Parmesan cheese

directions

- Dice garlic and mushrooms and set aside.

- Prepare linguini based on package directions.

- Heat a non-stick skillet with olive oil. Add garlic, cook until fragrant. Add mushrooms and sauté until softened. Set aside.

- Drain pasta, but save 1 cup of pasta water for the final dish.

- Assemble all ingredients in a serving bowl using half the Parmesan cheese. Add pasta water if mixture seems dry. Top with remaining Parmesan and serve with your favorite green salad.

Nutrition Facts	
Serves 4	
Amount Per Serving	
Calories	330
	% Daily Value*
Total Fat 12.5g	16%
Cholesterol 3.6mg	1%
Sodium 165.4mg	7%
Total Carbohydrate 44g	16%
Sugars 2.1g	
Protein 10.3g	21%

✦*recipe notes*✦

A harmonious combination of linguini, fragrant pesto, and earthy shitake mushrooms makes up this memorable pasta dish. Serve with your favorite green salad.

Parmesan Italian Oven-Crusted Potatoes

SERVINGS: 4   PREP TIME: 5 MIN   COOK TIME: 60 MIN

WINE PAIRING:

 Pine Ridge *Chenin Blanc Viognier*

 Theopolis *Petite Syrah*

ingredients

5 medium Yukon Gold potatoes
1/4 cup grated Parmesan cheese

2 tbsp olive oil
2 tsp Italian dry salad dressing mix

directions

- Preheat oven to 350F*. Cover a baking sheet with parchment paper.

- Wash and cut potatoes (skin on) in wedges and set aside in a bowl.

- In a separate bowl, mix remaining ingredients. Add to potatoes, toss well, and transfer to baking pan.

- Bake until golden brown and tender.

Nutrition Facts	
Serves 4	
Amount Per Serving	
Calories	288
	% Daily Value*
Total Fat 8.7g	11%
Cholesterol 3.6mg	1%
Sodium 101.2mg	4%
Total Carbohydrate 47.3g	17%
Sugars 2.3g	
Protein 7.5g	15%

✦*recipe notes*✦

These crispy oven-baked potatoes with a golden Parmesan crust create a delightful side dish or appetizer.

Ginger Carrots

SERVINGS: 4   PREP TIME: 15 MIN   COOK TIME: 30 MIN

WINE PAIRING:

 Veuve Clicquot *Champagne*

○ **McBride Sisters** *Sparkling Rose'*

ingredients

6-8 carrots, peeled
1 tsp sugar
1/4 tsp all-spice
1/4 tsp ground ginger
1 tbsp butter

For the Drizzle:
1/2 tsp vanilla
1 tsp honey

directions

- Pare the carrots with a knife or peeler and julienne cut.

- In a medium-sized skillet heat butter on low heat, add carrots, and increase heat to medium-high. Sprinkle carrots with sugar, all-spice, and ginger. Cover. Stir frequently until carrots are tender. Approximately 10 minutes.

- Remove cover and add vanilla and honey, increase heat to high and brown. Be careful not to burn.

- Remove from the heat and serve as an amazing side dish.

Nutrition Facts	
Serves 4	
Amount Per Serving	
Calories	116
	% Daily Value*
Total Fat 3.3g	4%
Cholesterol 7.6mg	3%
Sodium 133.1mg	6%
Total Carbohydrate 21.2g	8%
Sugars 11.7g	
Protein 1.8g	4%

✦*recipe notes*✦

Tender carrots infused with zesty ginger, deliver a delightful twist to a classic vegetable side dish. This is a pretty side dish and goes well with a garlic-based protein dish.

Yellow Rice and Golden Raisins

| SERVINGS: 4 | PREP TIME: 5 MIN | COOK TIME: 25 MIN |

WINE PAIRING:

◯ **Maison Noir OPP** *Pinot Gris*

◯ **Louis Jadot** *Gamay*

ingredients

2 cups water
1 cup rice (use basmati)
1 tbsp Blue Mountain Curry Powder

1 tbsp butter
Garlic Salt
1/2 cup golden raisins
2 stalks green onions chopped

directions

- Bring water, butter, and spices to a brisk boil in a 1-quart pot. Add rice and cover.

- Cook until all water is absorbed and the rice is tender.

- Remove from heat and add raisins, mix well and cover until ready to serve.

- Top with green onions and serve.

Nutrition Facts

Serves 4

Amount Per Serving	
Calories	258
	% Daily Value*
Total Fat 3.3g	4%
Cholesterol 7.6mg	3%
Sodium 160.2mg	7%
Total Carbohydrate 53.7g	20%
Sugars 12.3g	
Protein 4.1g	8%

✦*recipe notes*✦

Enjoy this fragrant yellow curry rice with bursts of sweetness from golden raisins. You may substitute your favorite curry powder. This goes well with sauteed cabbage and fried fish or chicken. Yummy!

Fried Green Bananas with Spicy Garlic Aioli Sauce

SERVINGS: 4-6   PREP TIME: 30 MIN   COOK TIME: 30 MIN

WINE PAIRING:

Newton *Chardonnay*

Daou Pessimist *Red Blend*

ingredients

3 ripe green bananas
1/2 tsp salt
3 cups water
Juice from 1/2 lime
Coconut oil for frying

For Spicy Garlic Aioli:
3 garlic cloves minced
2 tbsp olive oil
1 tsp malt vinegar
2 tbsp mayonnaise
Hot sauce to taste

directions

- Peel bananas and slice cross-wise (about 1/2 inch thick).

- Combine water, salt, and lime in a bowl. Add the bananas and let set while you prepare the sauce.

- **For Spicy Garlic Aioli Sauce:**
  - Mix garlic and olive oil. Let stand for 15 minutes. Add remaining ingredients, mix well, and let stand in refrigerator for at least 15 minutes. You can make this way ahead of time.
  - Drain and dry bananas. Fry in a medium skillet in coconut oil, browning on each side. Lay fried bananas on a paper towel to remove the excess oil. While hot, flatten bananas and sprinkle with salt.

Nutrition Facts	
Serves 4	
Amount Per Serving	
Calories	381
	% Daily Value*
Total Fat 31.5g	40%
Cholesterol 5.8mg	2%
Sodium 412.8mg	18%
Total Carbohydrate 28.1g	10%
Sugars 12.2g	
Protein 1.9g	4%

✦*recipe notes*✦

These green bananas burst with garlic. This is a great appetizer with a spicy sauce that pairs well with big wines.

Spicy Grilled Summer Squash

SERVINGS: 4   PREP TIME: 10 MIN   COOK TIME: 20 MIN

WINE PAIRING:

 Angeline *Rose'*

 Campo Viejo *Granacha*

ingredients

1 large yellow squash
1 large green squash
1 tbsp olive oil

1 (6 oz) can diced tomato and green chiles
Salt and pepper to taste

directions

- Wash squash and cut into half moons.

- Separate juice from tomato and green chiles. Set tomatoes and green chiles aside.

- Place squash in a bowl and add tomato/green chiles juice. Let stand for 10 minutes. Then drain off liquid.

- Grill on medium heat until al dente. Transfer to serving dish and top with tomatoes and green chiles.

Nutrition Facts	
Serves 4	
Amount Per Serving	
Calories	39
	% Daily Value*
Total Fat 3.6g	5%
Cholesterol 0mg	0%
Sodium 200.3mg	9%
Total Carbohydrate 2g	1%
Sugars 1.3g	
Protein 0.5g	1%

✦*recipe notes*✦

Fire up the grill for perfectly seasoned and spicy summer squash that will pair with your favorite grilled fish and meats.

Baby Spinach & Beet Salad with Lemongrass Dressing

SERVINGS: 4   PREP TIME: 10 MIN   COOK TIME: 0 MIN

WINE PAIRING:

 Matua Sauvignon Blanc

 Forrester Port

ingredients

For the Salad:
4 cups baby spinach
2 cooked beets cubed
1/3 small red onion, sliced
1/4 cup blue cheese crumbles

For the Dressing:
1 tbsp olive oil
1/2 tbsp rice vinegar
1 tsp lemongrass paste
1/2 tsp honey
salt and pepper to taster

directions

- Wash and spin spinach. Set aside.

- Prepare cubed beets and slice onions. Set aside.

- In a your salad bowl, mix all dressing ingredients together and let sit until you are ready to serve.

- To serve, add spinach and onions to dressing. Coat thoroughly. Separate into four servings, top with beets and Blue Cheese crumbles.

Nutrition Facts	
Serves 4	
Amount Per Serving	
Calories	78
	% Daily Value*
Total Fat 3.7g	5%
Cholesterol 0mg	0%
Sodium 257.5mg	11%
Total Carbohydrate 9.2g	3%
Sugars 5.8g	
Protein 2.1g	4%

✦ *recipe notes* ✦

A refreshing salad featuring vibrant baby spinach, beets, and a zesty lemongrass dressing. This salad is great with nuts and your favorite protein on top.

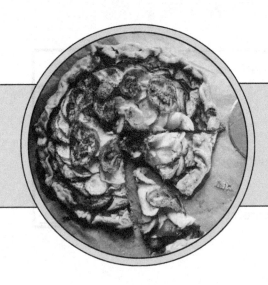

Eggplant Tart

SERVINGS: 4   PREP TIME: 30 MIN   COOK TIME: 90 MIN

WINE PAIRING:

 Albrecht Gewürztraminer

 Spier Pinotage

ingredients

2 large plum tomatoes
1 medium red onion
1/2 yellow squash
1/3 medium eggplant
3 cloves garlic

1 cup ricotta cheese
1/2 cup Parmesan cheese
1 Pillsbury refrigerated pie crust
10 Kalamata olives
2 tbsp olive oil

directions

- Preheat oven to 350*F

- Slice the eggplant and yellow squash crosswise into thin slices and then cut in half. Slice tomatoes in thin slices, Kalamata olives in half, and red onions into thin slices, halved. Drizzle with 1 tbsp of olive oil and set vegetables aside.

- Mix ricotta, minced garlic, and Parmesan cheese well. Spoon onto pie crust on a large baking sheet about 1/2 inch from the edge. Salt and pepper.

- Prepare tart by layering the eggplant in a circular fashion around the pie working from the outside towards the middle until the entire crust is covered. Layer the squash and onion next, then the tomatoes, and top with the olives.

- Fold the edges of the pie crust over the vegetables and pinch to hold in the filling. Drizzle with remaining olive oil. Bake for 1 hour and 15 minutes or until the crust is golden and the vegetables are soft. Allow to cool for 5 minutes before serving.

Nutrition Facts

Serves 4

Amount Per Serving

Calories	438

	% Daily Value*
Total Fat 26.6g	34%
Cholesterol 38.8mg	13%
Sodium 539.4mg	23%
Total Carbohydrate 36.9g	13%
Sugars 2.3g	
Protein 13.3g	27%

✦ *recipe notes* ✦

This savory eggplant tart with a flaky crust showcases the versatility of these beloved vegetables. This is a perfect brunch or light dinner recipe. Yummy!

Empanadas with Beef Crumbles (Vegetarian)

SERVINGS: 6   PREP TIME: 15 MIN   COOK TIME: 45 MIN

WINE PAIRING:

 Phebus Torrontes

Montes Carmenere

ingredients

1 package refrigerated Pillsbury pie crust (2 pie crusts)
1 package ground beef or Yves ground soy meat
1 egg
2 tbsp marinara sauce
2 tsp red pepper flakes

2 cloves garlic
2 tbsp Bajan Seasoning
1 small onion
1/2 cup milk

directions

- Preheat oven to 350 *.

- In a large skillet, brown the soy meat or ground beef over medium heat. Drain off any excess water or grease. Add the onion and garlic to the skillet and cook until softened.

- Stir in the marinara sauce, Bajan Seasoning, red pepper flakes and milk. Bring to a simmer and cook for 5 minutes.

- Roll out the pie crust, cut into equal pieces about 4 inches in diameter, Pour the filling into the prepared pie crust on one half, fold and pinch outer edges so filling won't seep out. place on a non stick baking sheet. Mix egg and brush each empanada on top.

- Bake for 30 to 35 minutes, or until the crust is golden brown and the filling is bubbly. Let cool for a few minutes before serving.

Nutrition Facts

Serves 6

Amount Per Serving

Calories	508
	% Daily Value*
Total Fat 29.4g	38%
Cholesterol 70.7mg	24%
Sodium 2888.3mg	126%
Total Carbohydrate 44.8g	16%
Sugars 3.7g	
Protein 15.3g	31%

✦ recipe notes ✦

These deliciously stuffed empanadas can be filled with savory beef or chicken or vegan meat crumbles. Great appetizer during football season or take on the beach in your beach bag.

Garlic and Truffle Mashed Cauliflower

SERVINGS: 6   PREP TIME: 10 MIN   COOK TIME: 30 MIN

WINE PAIRING:

 Bartenura Muscato

 Massolino Dolcetto

ingredients

1 large head of fresh cauliflower
1 tsp garlic powder
1 tbsp truffle oil

Salt and pepper
1 tbsp butter or garlic butter

directions

- Place cauliflower in a two-quart pot and cover bottom with water. Add salt, pepper, and garlic powder. Steam on medium-high until cauliflower is tender. About 10 minutes.

- Drain thoroughly. Place cauliflower in a food processor, bullet or mixer. Add butter and truffle oil. Blend until smooth and creamy.

Nutrition Facts	
Serves 6	
Amount Per Serving	
Calories	50
	% Daily Value*
Total Fat 4.4g	6%
Cholesterol 5.1mg	2%
Sodium 108.8mg	5%
Total Carbohydrate 2.7g	1%
Sugars 1.1g	
Protein 1.1g	2%

✦ *recipe notes* ✦

This creamy mashed cauliflower is infused with the rich flavors of garlic and truffle, making it a sophisticated side dish. Serve as a side or top with vegetables or any protein.

Grilled Corn Hash

SERVINGS: 6   PREP TIME: 20 MIN   COOK TIME: 30 MIN

WINE PAIRING:

○ **Kris** *Pinot Blanc*

◍ **Cusumano** *Nero d' Avola*

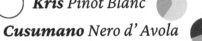

ingredients

2 ears fresh corn
1 small sweet red pepper
1 small sweet orange pepper

1 small yellow onion
3 garlic cloves
Olive oil

directions

- Preheat grill and turn down to medium heat.

- Shuck corn and set aside. Chop peppers and onion into small pieces and add to corn. Mince garlic and add to vegetables. Pour two tablespoons of olive oil on the vegetables and mix thoroughly.

- Grill vegetables on the grill on medium heat until lightly browned and the aroma of garlic and sugar from corn are prevalent.

Nutrition Facts	
Serves 6	
Amount Per Serving	
Calories	76
	% Daily Value*
Total Fat 3.1g	4%
Cholesterol 0mg	0%
Sodium 8.9mg	0%
Total Carbohydrate 12g	4%
Sugars 4.5g	
Protein 2g	4%

✦ *recipe notes* ✦

A smoky and satisfying hash made with grilled corn, perfect for brunch or a side dish with your BBQ.

Parmesan and Spicy Garlic Cauliflower Appetizer

WINE PAIRING:

 Buttercream Chardonnay

 **Radius** Merlot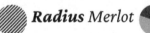

ingredients

1 head fresh cauliflower florets
3 cloves garlic minced
1/2 cup of olive oil
Optional: mix roasted garlic oil and
regular olive oil, half and half)

For the topping:
1 cup of shredded Parmesan cheese
1/4 cup bread crumbs
1/4 teaspoon red pepper flakes

directions

- Preheat oven to 350*F. Cover a large baking sheet with parchment paper.

- Mix garlic and oil in one bowl and set aside.

- In a separate bowl, add the topping ingredients.

- Cut and break apart cauliflower into small florets. Dip cauliflower florets into garlic oil and then into Parmesan mixture and place on parchment-covered baking sheet pan.

- Bake for 30 minutes until golden brown.

Nutrition Facts	
Serves 4	
Amount Per Serving	
Calories	389
	% Daily Value*
Total Fat 34g	44%
Cholesterol 22mg	7%
Sodium 495.1mg	22%
Total Carbohydrate 16.4g	6%
Sugars 4.5g	
Protein 10.1g	20%

✦*recipe notes*✦

Irresistible bite-sized cauliflower appetizers with a zingy garlic kick. This is garlic yummy!

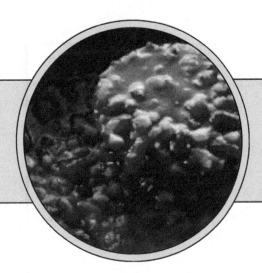

Vegetarian Chili with Honey Cornbread

SERVINGS: 6-8   PREP TIME: 15 MIN   COOK TIME: 120 MIN

WINE PAIRING:

Theopolis *Symphony*
Conundrum *Red Blend*

ingredients

2 Impossible Burger meats
1 (15 oz) can black beans, rinsed and drained
1 package McCormick Chili Seasoning
1/2 tsp cumin
1 (15 oz) can kidney beans, rinsed and drained
1 (15 oz) can pigeon peas beans, rinsed and drained
2 plum tomatoes, cubed

6 cloves garlic, minced
1/4 small hot pepper, chopped
1/2 cup red pepper, chopped
1/2 cup green pepper, chopped
1 large onion, chopped
1 (12 oz) can tomato paste
1 cup water

directions

- Heat slow cooker or crock pot on high.

- Dice onions, garlic, hot pepper, and green and red peppers. Set aside. Cube plum tomatoes into small (1/4 inch) pieces and set aside.

- Saute onions, green and red peppers, garlic, hot pepper (remove seeds for less heat), and crumbled "Impossible" meat on medium heat until you smell the garlic. Season with salt, pepper, and cumin. Remove from heat, add McCormick chili packet, stir, and set aside.

- Place beans, tomatoes, and veggie/meat mixture into the pot and stir. Add tomato paste and a cup of water, stir, cover, and cook for 2 hours or until beans are tender.

Nutrition Facts

Serves 6

Amount Per Serving

Calories	372
	% Daily Value*
Total Fat 11.6g	15%
Cholesterol 0mg	0%
Sodium 815.5mg	35%
Total Carbohydrate 47.3g	17%
Sugars 6.9g	
Protein 24.7g	49%

✦ *recipe notes* ✦

The most comforting dinner you could ever have. Serve with Honey Cornbread.

CHAPTER 8:

Cheers to Creative Cocktail Concoctions!

Cocktail Tools make it easy to create great cocktails like the pros. Some of these tools can be found right in your kitchen cabinet and cookware drawers but you may need to invest in a few. This chapter will walk you through the basics and have you making tasty cocktails immediately.

Let's start with the preparation of the must-haves.

- You will need a shot glass. Go find that souvenir one that you shoved away in your cabinet from years ago.
- Essential is a cocktail shaker. They come in many different sizes, but I like one that will make one or two cocktails. It makes it easy to manage the ingredients.
- Next, add a zester to your tool kit. You probably already have one if you are a big cook.
- Finally, find the juicer in your kitchen drawer. Remember the old one passed down from your grandmother.

Cocktail Cordials and Bitters are essential for making great cocktails. These basic ingredients are the foundation of most cocktails. Have them in your kitchen to make tasty cocktails immediately.

Whether you like sweet or savory these essentials will make you feel like a pro.

First, let's start with **simple syrup**. It's just sugar and water. You can buy it! Or you can make your own.

Simple Syrup Recipe

One part water and equal part sugar. Put a cup of each in a sauce pan. Heat on medium until the sugar melts and thickens a little. Place in a container and store in the refrigerator.

Here's your Cordials shopping list!

Finally, the fresh stuff to create palate rim teasers:

Cordials Shopping List
• Simple Syrup • Rose's Lime • Grenadine • Triple Sec • Angostura Bitters

Palate Rim Teasers
• Limes • Lemons • Oranges • Sugar • Sea salt

These quick tips will set you up to make yummy cocktails.

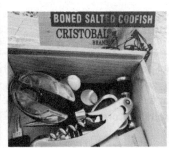

Jekyll and Hyde Martini

Ingredients

Serves 1

1 shot Jack Daniel's whiskey
1/2 shot Jekyll & Hyde licorice liqueur
1/4 lime (juice squeezed)
1/2 shot Simple Syrup

Procedure

- Add all ingredients in a martini shaker with ice. Shake until shaker is frosty. Pour into martini glass.
- Garnish with a lime wedge.

Manhattan SB

Ingredients

Serves 1

1 shot of whiskey (use your favorite)
1/2 shot of Luxardo Maraschino Liqueur
2 Maraschino cherries
1 orange peel

Procedure

- Start with a highball glass; add one large cube of ice.
- In a shaker of ice, add the whiskey and liqueur and shake well.
- Pour drink over the ice cube, twist orange peel, and add to drink. Top with 2 cherries

Orange Mash

Ingredients

Serves 1

1 shot Jack Daniel's whiskey
1/2 shot Grand Marnier
1/2 shot Simple Syrup
2 spritz of lemon juice
1/8 juice of a large orange
Half slice orange garnish
2 drops of Angostura

Procedure

- Mix all ingredients except orange garnish and Angostura in a shaker. Shake until frost appears.
- Pour in a highball glass, and add ice from the shaker.
- Top with orange and Angostura

Hot Apple Cider ala Stephanie

Ingredients

Serves 4

32 oz of fresh apple cider
4 sticks of cinnamon
1 tsp of nutmeg
2 shots Uncle Nearest Whiskey

Procedure

- Place cider, cinnamon, and nutmeg in a large saucepan and bring to a quick simmer on high heat. Reduce heat to low and simmer for 15 minutes.
- Pour 8 oz of cider into 4 mugs, add one cinnamon stick from the cooked cider and 1/2 shot of Uncle Nearest to each.
- Serve warm. Enjoy!

Muddled Mint Whiskey Sour

Ingredients

Serves 1
1 shot Uncle Nearest Whiskey
1 shot Cointreau
1/2 shot lemon juice
6 drops ginger bitters
Mint leaves

Procedure

- Muddle 2-3 mint leaves in a martini or high ball glass.
- Combine all ingredients except mint in a shaker.
- Shake until cold and pour on top of muddled fresh mint.
- Top with a mint leaf.

Sipping Sense Spiked Tea

Ingredients

Serves 1
1 shot Uncle Nearest Whiskey
1 shot Rooibos Tea
1/2 shot Cointreau
1/2 shot Simple Syrup
Juice from 1/4 lemon
Angostura Bitters for topping

Procedure

- Place all ingredients except bitters in a shaker of ice. Shake until frost appears on the shaker.
- Pour into a high ball glass. Add a few ice cubes from the shaker.
- Top with bitters and garnish with a lemon wedge.

Pink Mamma Martini

Ingredients

Serves 1

1 shot Tequila Reposado
1/2 shot Simple Syrup
Splash pink grapefruit juice
1/4 lime juice
1 tbsp sugar for glass rim (optional)
2 oz ginger ale (For VIRGIN option)

Procedure

- Spread sugar evenly on a saucer. Cut a small piece of lime, line the rim of the martini glass. Turn the glass rim upside down onto the sugar and coat the rim of the glass. Set aside.
- Combine tequila, Simple Syrup, and remaining juice from 1/4 squeezed lime into a cocktail shaker with ice.
- Shake the mixture until frost appears on outside surface of shaker.
- Remove the top of the shaker and pour the cocktail into martini glass. Top off the glass with a splash of pink grapefruit juice until your cocktail appears pink.
- For the VIRGIN version – Follow the recipe above, except substitute ginger ale for the tequila and mix/stir in the glass. DO NOT USE SHAKER.

Orange Ginger Blossom

Ingredients

Serves 1

1 shot of Tequila Reposado
1/2 shot of Grand Marnier
1/2 shot Simple Syrup
1/4 shot Real Lime juice
Juice from 1/4 orange
Orange for garnish
2 drops ginger bitters

Procedure

- Mix all ingredients except orange garnish and ginger bitters in a shaker. Shake until frost appears.
- Pour in a highball glass and add ice from the shaker.
- Top with orange and ginger bitters.

Pisco Sour

Ingredients

Serves 1
1 shot Pisco liquor
1/2 shot lime juice
1/3 shot Simple Syrup
1 egg white
4 drops of Angostura Bitters

Procedure

- Place all ingredients in a shaker half full of ice. Shake vigorously until frost appears on the shaker.
- Strain the cocktail into a martini glass. Drip 4 drops of bitters on top and serve.

Pisco Goblin

Ingredients

Serves 1
1 shot of Pisco
1/2 shot of Cointreau
1 shot Egg Nog
4 drops of Bitters (for taste and color)

Procedure

- Mix all ingredients except ginger bitters in a shaker. Shake until frost appears.
- Pour in a highball glass and add ice from the shaker.
- Top with Halloween decor/candy corn or a sprinkle of cinnamon and cinnamon stick. (Optional)
- Add Bitters drops.

CHAPTER 9

To Toasts, Tastings, and Table Settings!

Entertaining should be fun, not stressful. I have learned that you can make any hosting look and feel inviting for your guests with just a little thought. Whether you are pulling together a quick charcuterie tray or a formal sit-down dinner, having "go-to" ready pieces can make this easy.

One of the many wonderful memories from my years of friendship with Divas Uncorked was the illuminating tabletops created for our wine dinners and private tastings. These decorating ideas became known as "diva style."

The decorating divas were extremely passionate about the designs they dreamed up. So much so that suggestions from outside the team were often dismissed. The rest of the divas would run away when it came time for the work, fearful of being scolded for not following orders. We had a lot of fun adding corks, grapes in all forms, sizes, and materials, and flowing fabrics to our tables at each event. We didn't have a lot of money to spend, but collectively we had a lot of stuff from each other's personal collections that we would lug in boxes and tubs to each event.

One of my most memorable displays was at one of our first public wine dinners. It was winter in New England so we called the dinner "Winter Wonderland." Imagine a hotel ballroom filled with glass candle holders of all shapes and sizes with white tapered candles and votives. The decorating divas even found glass grapes. To create the ambiance, the team asked the hotel staff to spot each table. We had hotel staff up on ladders moving spots over 20 tables. When guests walked into this dimly lit ballroom all you could hear were the wows, oohs, and ahs. It was just breathtaking to see.

So much of entertaining with food and wine is about the experience and I learned so much from our decorating divas. It was always a surprise and great fun to watch our venues transformed by the imaginations of my friends.

My grandmother made a table beautiful with her hand-sewn table linens. I have been collecting entertaining items my whole adult life. One of these days I will run out of room to store things. I love my passed-down china, flatware, and platters, my bargain second-hand store finds, and the discount store clearance rack items. With these treasures, I can make any table pop. Don't be afraid to mix and match textures, styles, and colors. Guests love a little creativity. And don't forget flowers on a plate and candles at each place setting. These little extra touches warm up any party or formal dining setting.

Decorating, making the serving of food, wine, and cocktails look approachable and appealing, can usually be accomplished for little cost and many times by using what you have around the house already. Stores such as Marshalls, TJ MAXX, Homesense, and At Home offer lots of decorating and entertaining items for under ten dollars all day long.

Here are three menus and visual ideas you can copy to have your guests compliment your skills after sharing a hospitality experience with you.

Impromptu Cocktail Party

During the summer I find myself entertaining impromptu all the time, so I keep a few things on hand to make a quick cocktail menu look like I had hours to prepare.

Serving Items:
Pick up these items in the markdown rack or bin of your favorite home store every time you see them.

- Cocktail napkins
- Cocktail napkin holder
- Reusable appetizer forks or toothpicks
- Reusable appetizer plates
- Serving pieces like odds and ends bowls and plates made from your old tableware set, cutting boards, cake plates and spreaders.

Food, Wine, and/or Spirits Suggestions:

Depending on your company's preference, you may only need wine on hand, but if you have the items to make cocktails (see Chapter 10) you are all set no matter the ask. You can keep unopened red and white in the fridge for these moments.

- Two cheese types
- Crackers or make some garlic bread bites with hamburger or hotdog buns
- Chips (any type)
- Some type of spread like a spicy jelly, fig jam, jarred pesto, or dip
- Olives
- Pepperoni
- Carrots
- Celery
- Wine

These are a few suggestions and you don't need them all. But a combination of a few will allow you to set out tasty bites quickly and easily for your guests.

Casual Dinner for 4

A quick casual dinner should take no longer than 45 minutes to prepare. This can be accomplished in the oven, on the stovetop, or grill with the right foods. Foods such as pasta, all types of salad greens, chicken, fish, or root vegetables will make a quick, healthy, and wine-friendly meal.

Casual dinner to me means using your everyday dishes and flatware. Choose a nice set of wine glassware and cloth napkins and rings you have on hand to pretty up a casual table and you will be all set. Here are a few ideas that will have you prepared in a pinch.

Serving Items:
Pick up these items in the markdown rack or bin of your favorite home store every time you see them.

- Cloth napkins for all seasons
- Napkin rings
- Pasta serving dish
- All-purpose serving platter

Casual Dinner for 4

FOOD AND WINE SUGGESTIONS

Parmesan Chicken with grilled or roasted vegetables
Roasted Tomato and Kale Clam Sauce with Spaghetti
Red Lentil Pasta with Smoked Salmon and Peas
Ceasar Salad and Baked Fish

WHITE WINE IDEAS

Sauvignon Blanc
Riesling

RED WINE IDEAS

Pinot Noir
Malbec

Formal Dinner

A formal dinner is the time to shine. What food you choose for serving will depend on the occasion. Many times we set out on this path for the holiday seasons, special birthdays or celebrations such as anniversaries, graduations and out of town visitors. There are many ideas in the numerous recipes in this cookbook. Formal dinner for me is more about how you deliver the meal than what you serve.

This can be accomplished with many items you already have in your cabinets. You can use many of the items from our casual dinner lists. But a formal dinner set up should look closer to this diagram.

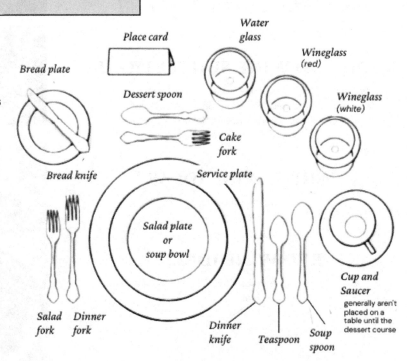

Place card

Water glass

Wineglass (red)

Bread plate

Dessert spoon

Wineglass (white)

Cake fork

Bread knife

Service plate

Salad plate or soup bowl

Cup and Saucer
generally aren't placed on a table until the dessert course

Salad fork   Dinner fork

Dinner knife   Teaspoon   Soup spoon

You don't have to have all these pieces of glassware, flatware, or dinnerware on your table, but you should follow the proper placement. Here are some ideas and images to help you look like a pro.

Serving Items:

Pick up these items in the markdown rack or bin of your favorite home store every time you see them.

- Cloth napkins for all seasons
- Napkin rings
- Multiple sizes of glassware (they don't need to match)
- Interesting dessert and salad plates (you can mix them with your everyday dinnerware)

Table Manners 101

1 Place your napkin in your lap as soon as you're seated.

2 When serving wine to your guests, taste it first before serving them to make sure the wine is not spoiled.

3 Do not begin eating your meal until everyone at the table is served or your host gives you permission.

4 Once you use your knife, never lay it back on the table; place it across the upper right-hand corner of your plate.

5 Once you have completed your meal, place your knife and fork in a closed position in the middle of your plate. This alerts your server or host that you are done.

154

Acknowledgments

This book of favorite recipes is dedicated to my mother and grandmother. They will both always be in my heart for sharing their love of cooking and entertaining and their skills with me.

My inspiration for Sipping Sense, Uncorking the Flavors of Wine, Entertaining, and Healthy Cooking came from B. Smith's "Entertaining and Cooking for Friends" cookbook (1995). I had the pleasure of meeting her in 1998. She was my Martha Stewart and her success has stuck with me all these years.

A special "thank you" to the women of Divas Uncorked (Carole Alkins, Barbara Cruz, Gert Cowan, Carolyn Hebsgaard, Katherine Kennedy, Karen Ward, Paula Wright, the late Rosalind Johnson) who expanded my skills on how to entertain with style. During our years of sharing wine together either privately or at our public events, the Divas creatively exceeded table design boundaries and decorated our events in what became known as "Diva Style". Thank you for always pushing the envelope of what makes pretty happen.

A heartfelt thank you to my husband Basil and daughter Desiree for being my taste testers on all things food. They have never complained even when I am sure I did not deliver my best work.

Thank you to all my friends and collaborators who continuously encourage me to be my best self. You have supported all my creative wine endeavors over the years. I would not be motivated without everyone pushing me beyond what I even think is possible at times.

Finally, my collaborator and book designer, Joana Marie Ballera has been an amazing partner. She is creative, exceptional with color and style, and very thoughtful when giving feedback. This book is our SUCCESS.

Recipe and Topic Index

Entertaining

Veggies/Vegetarian

Fish and Seafood

Wine Tips

Made in the USA
Monee, IL
08 October 2024

67420121R00092